D1567953

Original edition published in 2001 by
Libri de Hispania, Littleton, Colorado
© 2001 by Janice Bennett

New edition printed by permission of Janice Bennett

Design by Paul Cooper

Published in 2005 by Ignatius Press, San Francisco
ISBN 1–58617–111–9
Library of Congress control number 2005924734
Printed in China

SACRED BLOOD, SACRED IMAGE

THE SUDARIUM OF OVIEDO

New Evidence for the Authenticity of The Shroud of Turin

JANICE BENNETT

IGNATIUS PRESS   SAN FRANCISCO

FOR MY HUSBAND, JIM,
OUR CHILDREN SCOTT AND ANNE,
AND IN MEMORY OF MY PARENTS,
HARRY AND DOROTHY GOODMAN

CONTENTS

ILLUSTRATIONS

Cover: Superimposition of the bloodstains of the Sudarium of Oviedo on the image found on the Shroud of Turin. A drop of blood appears over the left eyebrow of the Man of the Sudarium that is different from the blood of the principal stains. Its parallelism with the drop on the Shroud of Turin seems to indicate that it comes from the same wound. *Courtesy, Centro Español de Sindonología (C.E.S.).*

Back cover: The Holy Chest of relics, found in the Holy Chamber of the Cathedral of Oviedo, Spain. The silver plating is engraved in Latin, "Of the Sepulcher of the Lord and of His Sudarium and of His Most Holy Blood." *Courtesy, C.E.S.*

1. Historical odyssey of the Holy Sudarium of Oviedo from Jerusalem to Oviedo, Spain. *Courtesy, C.E.S.*
2. San Salvador, the Cathedral of Oviedo in Asturias, Spain. *Jim Bennett.*
3. The *Cámara Santa,* or Holy Chamber, of the Cathedral of Oviedo. *Courtesy, C.E.S.*
4. Benediction with the Sudarium of Oviedo on September 14, 1999.
5.a. The lower hermitage on Monsacro, the sacred mountain where it is believed that the relics were kept for fifty years.
5.b. Our Lady of Monsagro, the upper hermitage on Monsacro.
6.a. Close view of Our Lady of Monsagro, medieval hermitage where the relics of Oviedo were hidden in the "Well of St. Toribio."
6.b. Interior of the Hermitage of Our Lady of Monsagro. The "Well of St. Toribio" can be seen on the right.
7.a. Monastery of St. Toribio of Liébana in Picos de Europa.
7.b. The relic of the True Cross, exposed for veneration in its gold casing.
8. Altar in which the relic of the True Cross is safeguarded.
9. Engraving of the year 1722, the work of Gaspar Massi, which shows St. Toribio, Bishop of Astorga, holding the True Cross, with the Monastery and its surroundings in the background.
10.a. Photograph of one of the many types of pollen found on the Sudarium. *Courtesy, C.E.S.*
10.b. Photograph of aloe and myrrh, found attached to the blood, indicating that they were applied to the cloth before the blood had dried completely. *Courtesy, C.E.S.*
11.a. Obverse side of the Sudarium, as it is currently being shown to the public. *Courtesy, C.E.S.*

11.b. Reverse side of the Sudarium. The left reverse stain was in direct contact with the face. *Courtesy, C.E.S.*

12. Diagonal folds on the Sudarium, and on a model used for comparison. They indicate that the linen was knotted in one corner when the cloth was wrapped in the second position.

13. Speculated inversion. The "Principal Stain 1" is that which was in contact with the face, and appears inverted as in a mirror. *Courtesy, C.E.S.*

14. The principal stain of the left reverse side of the cloth, that was in contact with the face. The outline of the trapezoidal stain is evident surrounding the area that corresponds to the nose and mouth. Within this area the finger-shaped stains are outlined on both sides of the mouth and the lower part of the nose. The forehead stain can be seen to the upper right of the burn hole. *Courtesy, C.E.S.*

15.a. The lower part of the principal stain is formed with the body in a vertical position. *Courtesy, C.E.S.*

15.b. The upper part of the principal stain is formed with the body in a horizontal position. *Courtesy, C.E.S.*

16. Positions of the linen. The Sudarium was placed over the head, first when it was in a vertical position, and then when the body was placed horizontally on a flat surface. The final position shows how the cloth was left after being removed from the head. *Courtesy, C.E.S.*

17.a. The trapezoidal stain was generated by a left hand that applied pressure to the nasal area in order to contain the flow of blood. *Courtesy, C.E.S.*

17.b. Finger-shaped stains were formed when the same left hand, inverting its position, embraces the nose between the thumb and index finger, also to contain the blood flow. *Courtesy, C.E.S.*

18. Denominations of the major stains on the reverse side of the Sudarium. *Courtesy, C.E.S.*

19.a. Bust 1. Front view of how the bloodstains correspond to a human head in three dimensions. *Courtesy, C.E.S.*

19.b. Bust 2. Back view. *Courtesy, C.E.S.*

20. Comparison of the Sudarium of Oviedo and the Shroud of Turin. A clotted flow of blood appears on the right, extending the length of the beard. It is post-mortem blood on both linens, with a very similar morphology, measured at 1,310 mm^2 on the Shroud and 1,980 mm^2 on the Sudarium. *Courtesy, C.E.S.*

PREFACE

I would like to begin this work with an explanation of my involvement with the Holy Sudarium of Oviedo, currently being studied by the Investigative Team of the Spanish Center of Sindonology (EDICES), in Valencia, Spain, directed by Guillermo Heras Moreno.

Inspired by a trip to the Holy Land with a Hispanic group of pilgrims from Denver and enamored of their language, I decided to study Spanish in 1990. At the time I was in transition, having just ended ten years in typography and graphic design, and was also studying Sacred Scripture with the Catholic Biblical School of Denver. I continued my studies in Spanish until I received an M.A. in Spanish literature from the University of Colorado in Boulder in 1997. Especially during my first years of study, I avidly read a popular Spanish magazine called *¡Hola!*, and in the issue of December 2, 1993, I noticed a small article concerning the Holy Sudarium of the Cathedral of Oviedo. Although quite knowledgeable about the Shroud of Turin, the existence of another burial cloth of Jesus was unknown to me, and I read about the work being done by the Spanish Center of Sindonology with intense interest. During the coming years I searched fruitlessly for further information, and finally planned a trip to Oviedo, Spain, with my family in search of the cloth.

In December of 1996 we visited the Holy Chamber of the Cathedral, and of course, there was nothing to see. The guide explained to me everything he knew about the architecture of the chapel, the saints buried there, and the innumerable relics that are kept in the chest, without mentioning the Sudarium. At the time there wasn't even a photograph of the relic, and I was disappointed and confused, believing that I had somehow been mistaken about the location of the cloth. Only when I finally asked him where the relic was kept did he reply that it was in the silver chest along with the other relics.

This attitude of secrecy and protection seems to have characterized the permanence of the Sudarium in Oviedo throughout its history. While the treasury of relics in the Cathedral of Oviedo has always been a pilgrimage destination for the faithful and has been associated with indulgences for many centuries, the Sudarium itself has never been promoted or advertised. Perhaps one of the reasons is that, until the publication of the recent scientific studies, little has been known about this cloth or how it was used, and this is true for the historical sudarium mentioned in the Gospel of John, as well as for the Sudarium of Oviedo. In fact, during a recent trip to Oviedo for the benediction of September 14, 1999, one of the guides said that the cloth was a piece of the Shroud of Turin; another thought that it had received its stains from contact with the Shroud. At that point, neither had read the publications of CES. I have mentioned the cloth to several Spanish priests, and none had ever heard of it. While the rest of the world is beginning to hear a little about its existence, the Spanish are perhaps the least knowledgeable of all.

I am pleased to report that this situation is finally beginning to change. With the Photographic Exposition of the Sudarium, prepared by CES and in the Cathedral of San Salvador from February until October of the year 2000, visitors are now made aware of the importance of this relic. During my visit to the Cathedral in June of 2000, the guide, who I believe was the same gentleman who had failed to mention the Sudarium in 1996, was now considerably more knowledgeable.

In January of 1999 I discovered the web site of the Spanish Center of Sindonology, and from then on I have been involved in studying the information that has been published. I spoke with Dr. Jorge-Manuel Rodríguez, the vice-president of CES, in Valencia last June, and have been translating the work of EDICES for Dr. John Jackson of Colorado Springs, a member of the team since 1994. Rafael Somoano Berdasco, the Dean-President of the Chapter of the Cathedral of Oviedo, permitted me to see the cloth in the sacristy of the Cathedral after the blessing on September 14, one of only three days of the year when it is exposed. Other information I have gathered during my travels in Spain, particularly in Oviedo and at the Monastery of St. Toribio in Liébana, and from research done in the National Library of Madrid. I consider it a privilege to have been able to translate the work of this organization which, although tedious and quite difficult at times due to its technical language, has revealed so much new information about the passion and death of Jesus of Nazareth. I hope to present it in this book in a form that will make it accessible to the average reader, who probably does not have any particular knowledge about forensics, pollen studies, and Spanish history.

Sacred Blood, Sacred Image is written from the perspective of a Catholic who was captivated from the very first moment by the possibility that the Sudarium of Oviedo actually wrapped the head of Jesus, and who then undertook a rather long and passionate journey in search of information that might authenticate and explain this unknown relic that has always been believed to be the Sudarium of the Lord. As I have discovered, this is similar to what EDICES has ventured to accomplish, and the results of their research to date have been fascinating and extend far beyond my initial expectations. This investigative team, at least in the opinion of the author, has done an incredible and very thorough job, in spite of the fact that they believe that they have only just begun. I believe that this can be credited to their objectivity, competence, and ability to cooperate as a team, often sacrificing personal interests in favor of common goals.

I had been informed that the Sudarium would be exposed for the Millennium, just as the Shroud of Turin, an event that would have been a first in its history. This, however, has not come to pass, possibly due to fear for the security of this precious relic, or the possibility of contamination from the reconstruction and restoration project that has been initiated on the Cathedral. The Photographic Exposition, however, with text in Spanish, clearly manifests the highlights of the investigation of EDICES. Although the visitor to the Cathedral is only able to examine this informative display until October 22, it has also been published as a book that is available in English. Those who desire to actually see the cloth, however, must visit Oviedo on one of the three traditional days when it is removed from its chest for a public benediction: September 14 and 21, and Good Friday. As the reader will discover, tradition, propriety, and a profound respect for this priceless relic have always triumphed in the history of the Sudarium of Oviedo, and the Third Millennium is not likely to bring changes in favor of exploitation. The *Sudarium Domini*, or Sudarium of the Lord, will continue to be preserved in relative obscurity, as it has been for the last two thousand years, for future generations.

Janice Bennett
LITTLETON, COLORADO
AUGUST, 2000

INTRODUCTION

THE SUDARIUM OF OVIEDO AND THE BIRTH OF CES

Sacred Blood, Sacred Image: The title of this book refers to the two burial cloths of Jesus of Nazareth mentioned by John the Evangelist. One is saturated with the Sacred Blood of the Savior, a proclamation of His death on the cross. The second contains the divine imprint of the Risen One, a testimony to His Resurrection. The Shroud of Turin is well known, but the "other shroud" is not. Is it possible that the mysterious sudarium of Jesus to which John the Evangelist refers when speaking of his arrival at faith in the tomb is really the ancient, bloodstained cloth that has been venerated in the Cathedral of Oviedo, Spain, for so many centuries?

What exactly is the Sudarium of Oviedo? First of all, it can be said that it is an ancient linen cloth that has been in Spain since the seventh century and venerated in Oviedo for more than 1,200 years. It was originally a white linen cloth with a taffeta texture, now stained, dirty, and wrinkled. It is rectangular, somewhat irregular, and measures approximately 34 by 21 inches[1]. The principal bloodstains clearly form a mirror image along the axis formed by a fold that is still present. They are fundamentally light brown in color, in varying degrees of intensity. Although the linen has been traditionally called the "Holy Sudarium" or "Holy Face," there is no visible image of a face on the relic, only blood that is believed to be that of Jesus of Nazareth. The cloth has always been known as the *Sudarium Domini,* or the Sudarium of the Lord, even though no one really knows anything about the sudarium mentioned by

---

[1] 855 x 526 mm.

John, other than the fact that it was on the head of Jesus and was found by the apostles Peter and John in the tomb.

In spite of the fact that Oviedo became an important pilgrimage stop for those on their way to Santiago de Compostela to visit the remains of St. James, the Apostle, there has been no attempt to advertise the presence of the cloth in Oviedo. On the contrary, apart from a benediction given with the cloth three times a year in recent centuries, the cloth has been enclosed in a silver-plated chest throughout most of its permanence in the city. Few Spaniards know of its existence, and the rest of the world is just beginning to hear mention of it, due to the recent scientific studies of the investigative team of the Spanish Center of Sindonology, which have linked it to the Holy Shroud of Turin. Their studies have been published exclusively in Spanish, in 1996 and 1998, and until now only one small book has been published in English, that of Mark Guscin (1998), who primarily discusses its implications for the Shroud of Turin. While some may have heard of the cloth, the sources of information are few, and most are inaccessible to the English-speaking population. Apart from the researchers, the Chapter of the Cathedral of Oviedo, the Spanish Center of Sindonology, those attending the First International Congress on the Sudarium of Oviedo, and a few more individuals, almost no one knows anything of substance about the cloth.

As an example, two current books can be cited, one about relics, and the other concerning the Shroud of Turin. Joan Carroll Cruz, in her 1984 book[2], dedicates a page to the Sudarium of Oviedo, which reflects popular opinion about the relic prior to the work of EDICES. According to what she has written, some believed that the cloth was applied to the face of Jesus after He had been covered with the shroud, and others that it was used to support the jaw of Jesus. Neither of these theories is true according to the results of the investigative team, however, and added to this difficulty is the fact that, according to the same source, at least four churches in France and three in Italy claim portions of the grave cloths of Jesus. These may indeed be genuine articles that were used at some point during the transport of the body to the tomb, or during the burial itself. The scientists of the Holy Shroud of Turin Research Project have

---

[2] *Relics* (Huntington, Indiana: Our Sunday Visitor, Inc., 1984).

indicated the possible presence of a chin band tied around the face, but, as will be demonstrated in the discussion of the results of the investigation of EDICES, the Sudarium of Oviedo was not a chin band, and it has been confirmed that it was used to contain the flow of blood from the nose and mouth before the body was wrapped in a shroud.

The other mention of the Sudarium can be found in the 1998 book by Gino Moretto, *The Shroud: A Guide*. Under the section entitled "The Shroud of Turin and the Napkin of Oviedo" the author states that "according to an ancient tradition, the Sudarium was placed over the face of Jesus (already wrapped in the Shroud) after he had been taken down from the cross." Although he cites several of the conclusions of EDICES, the previously stated tradition is not clarified, which might lead the reader to believe that the Sudarium received its stains from the Shroud, or that this was its only function. On the contrary, EDICES has found that the cloth was wrapped around the head of a crucifixion victim while he was still on the cross, was re-wrapped after he had been placed in a horizontal position, remained in place while he was transported to a nearby location, and was then removed and placed aside. It could not have received its stains from contact with the Shroud, and most definitely did not remain in place underneath the Shroud.

When one visits the Cathedral of Oviedo, he or she is generally advised that there is a cloth there believed to be the Sudarium of Jesus of Nazareth. During my visit there in 1996, however, I was not informed until I asked the guide where it is kept, and during my visit for the benediction of September 14th, 1999, more than one priest walking in the vicinity of the cathedral told me that there is no blessing with the cloth on that date. They, of course, were misinformed. Nevertheless, a full-size facsimile of the cloth has since been placed in the Holy Chamber, and visitors are told what it is, but it is not given more or less importance than the other religious objects and relics in the room.

As mentioned in the Preface, I was surprised that in September of 1999 the guide announced to the visitors that the cloth was the largest piece of the Shroud in the world, and seemed to spend far more time enumerating and explaining the other relics, such as the sandal of St. Peter, the Cross of the Angels, the Cross of Victory, and the Cross of Nicodemus. Unless one comes to Oviedo specifically for the benediction, it is not possible to see the actual relic, and if one did, it would be impossible to decipher the bloodstains that appear on the linen. For the merely curious, it is hardly worth the trouble. On the other hand, if this cloth actually contains the physical remains of the blood of Jesus, as it certainly appears it does according to the initial studies, a pilgrimage to Oviedo would be the event of a lifetime, and it for this reason I feel that it is important to publish the information obtained by CES. Although it would be impossible to see the actual cloth apart from the three traditional dates, that does not detract from the spiritual value that might be gained from a visit at other times of the year. Medieval pilgrims crossed mountains on foot to visit the Cathedral of San Salvador, without any hope whatsoever that the chest would be opened, and while that may sound trite to the modern pilgrim who is able to fly to religious destinations without experiencing the least discomfort, it underscores the deep and profound respect that has always been shown toward the Sudarium. Precisely because it has always been believed to be the blood relic of Jesus, it has never been exploited. This is one of the strongest arguments in favor of its authenticity, apart from the scientific evidence.

The authors of *Hallazgos recientes* mention the narration of Ambrosio de Morales, commissioned by Philip II to inventory the relics of the Cathedral of Oviedo. Recorded in Madrid in 1765 by Antonio Marín, a translation of this account gives the reader an idea of the difficulty involved in comprehending the relic at first sight, particularly the type of information it contains:

> *The Holy Sudarium is a square, three-fourths of a yard in length and a half yardstick wide, all a little more or less. The linen is not very white, and although one scrutinizes it, one is surprised in a certain way for not being able to understand what it is. It has larger half-washed bloodstains, and lesser ones, in many areas: some say that in one of these great stains there is a representation of the face of our Redeemer, and of other particular things. What I saw, although I am unworthy, is that it attracts notable devotion, so that it enraptures in a certain way even a sinner like me.*

Two of the members of EDICES, the investigative team of the Spanish Center of Sindonology, are Guillermo Heras Moreno, an engineer and coordinator of EDICES, and José Delfín Villalaín Blanco, a doctor of medicine and vice-president of investigation of CES. They recall that they had once been in the same position as this visitor of long ago, having just arrived in Oviedo to begin their scientific investigation. Added to the difficulty of understanding the cloth by looking at it are added others, such as the medieval falsification of relics and even of the documents which refer to such relics, and especially the lack of information concerning the Sudarium of Jesus and how it was used. The only Biblical reference to this relic is made by the evangelist John, who makes the startling revelation in Chapter 20:5-9 that the position of the linens in the tomb is what led him to faith in the Resurrection.

The birth of the process of investigation that in the words of the EDICES "has only just begun," can be traced back to a visit to Oviedo in 1965, made by Mons. Guilio Ricci, an Italian priest and Shroud scholar. Ricci was searching for the "sudarium" mentioned in John 20:6-7. One presumes that his knowledge of Greek led him to understand that the Shroud is not the same type of linen that the evangelical "sudarium" would have to be, because the sudarium had been placed on the head of Jesus, while the shroud wrapped his body. Ricci knew that a linen called the "Holy Sudarium" existed in Oviedo, and resolved to examine the linen up close.

The results of his investigations were published in his books *L'Uomo della Síndone è Jesú* (Milan 1965) and in *La Síndone contestata, difesa, spiegata* (Rome 1992). He was the first to suggest a very notable correspondence between the stains of the linen of Oviedo and those found around the face which appears on the Shroud of Turin, and asked himself the question: If this linen was once on the body of Jesus of Nazareth, when and how was it utilized? The Gospel of John is the only one that mentions the presence of a sudarium in the sepulcher of Jesus, and doesn't give any explanation beyond saying that it was or had been on the head of Jesus. The tendency would be to relate it with the sudarium cited in the account of the resurrection of Lazarus (Jn. 11:14), but science has since proved that both cloths had different uses. CES maintains today that the stains of the Sudarium of Oviedo were produced after the death of the individual, and that it was removed immediately before the entire body was wrapped in a shroud. The sudarium of Lazarus was most likely a chin band, tied around the face and knotted at the top of the head. From studies done on the Shroud of Turin, it appears that there may also have been a chin band around the face of Jesus, underneath the Shroud; this cloth would also have been called a *sudarium*, a word that refers to any sweat or face cloth. As will be seen later, a *sudarium* had many possible uses, as a turban, towel, or scarf, in addition to funerary functions.

The publication of Ricci's work led to the formation of the present research team of the Sudarium of Oviedo. The Spanish Center of Sindonology (CES) was officially opened on December 18, 1987, after having solicited and obtained permission from the Chapter of the Cathedral of Oviedo. While they were taking the first steps to initiate a scientific multidisciplinary study on the sudarium, the news was made public that, according to the carbon 14 dating of the Shroud, it had been fabricated in the Middle Ages, between the years 1260 and 1390. For the investigative team, the following question immediately arose: If the Shroud and the Sudarium have bloodstains from the same person, how is it possible that the Shroud is from the cited era if the Sudarium has been in Oviedo since the eighth century and in Spain since the seventh century? In order to answer this question, they began their work on November 8 of 1989, the date when official permission was granted to carry out a complete, multidisciplinary study on the Sudarium.

The studies on the Sudarium of Oviedo have been continuous since their inception. EDICES is the center's investigative team, composed of approximately 40 members in various scientific fields. In the beginning this team was required to keep silent about their findings, until the First International Congress on the Sudarium of Oviedo was held there in 1994, which was followed by the publication in 1996 of the presentations that had been given, most of them in Spanish. As they have stated, the investigation has only just begun. Nevertheless, they have also said that their only interest in this investigation has been what it might reveal about the circumstances surrounding the passion, death, and resurrection of Jesus of Nazareth. If they had found one thing during these past eleven years that would have disproved the authenticity of the Sudarium of Oviedo, they would have immediately ended their studies. On the contrary, what has been found to date is quite fascinating, and completely in accordance with what we know about the death of Jesus.

PART ONE

THE HISTORY OF THE SUDARIUM OF OVIEDO

But in those times, it is known that many things occurred that are not written, as, for example, the linens and the sudarium in which the body of the Lord was wrapped. We read that it was found, but we do not read that it was preserved. Nevertheless, I do not believe that the relics would have been disregarded, but preserved for future times.

ST. BRAULIO OF ZARAGOZA, SPAIN (D. 651)

CHAPTER ONE

FROM JERUSALEM TO SPAIN: THE ODYSSEY OF THE RELICS

I t must be stated at the very beginning that this part of the investigation is the least developed, due to the destruction of important manuscripts, the remoteness of the times in which the cloth was brought to Spain, and the fact that no one has undertaken this task before now. An additional reason is that the Shroud and the Sudarium of Jesus have been confused throughout the ages, due to the fact that, although the sudarium is mentioned in the Gospel of John 20:5-7, its function is not clear in the Biblical passage. Artistically, the "Descent from the Cross" is never portrayed with a sudarium covering the head of the Lord, and the majority of books written about the Shroud hardly mention the existence of the head cloth. If they do, its usage is purely conjecture and often contradictory. Furthermore, it appears that there may have been two shrouds, one that covered the body of Jesus from the descent from the cross until his final entombment, and the "clean shroud" that wrapped his body in the tomb, according to the Gospels, traditionally believed to be the Shroud of Turin. The term *sudarium* has often been erroneously used to describe the first shroud, as occurs in the *Diccionario de la Real Academia Española*.

A sudarium is mentioned in the account of the raising of Lazarus, but in this case it seems to have wrapped his face in the manner of a chin band, underneath the shroud or linen strips that bound his body. Although the head of Jesus may have also been wrapped with a chin band, it appears that this is not the sudarium to which John refers, because John explicitly mentions that it had *covered* the head of Jesus, and that it was not with the other linens. John the Evangelist was an eyewitness of the events of the Crucifixion, and according to early tradition was the apostle John, the son of Zebedee and brother of

James. John was continually present at the foot of the cross during the passion and death of Jesus, and most probably accompanied the procession with the body to the sepulcher. As will be discussed later, the position of the burial cloths was extremely important to him, and has great significance because it is what brought him to faith in the Resurrection.

Due to lack of knowledge about the sudarium, it has often been confused with the Shroud, and this quandary has often made it difficult to identify early historical references to its veneration in Jerusalem. Although the history of the cloth may be mixed with some legendary material, its traditional route from Jerusalem to Alexandria in the north of Africa, and into Spain, is supported completely by the initial pollen studies of EDICES. Manuscripts are also being discovered which support the tradition of the passage of the cloth from Jerusalem to Spain, and although some questions still remain, they are beginning to be clarified. The investigation of the history of the cloth is ongoing, as is that of every area of study undertaken by the investigative team. In fact, several of the members are currently launching a thorough search for historical references to the Sudarium of Oviedo, and various interesting manuscripts have already been found, which will be discussed.

With that being said, the history of the odyssey of the cloth from Jerusalem to Spain is found in a number of manuscripts, among them the chronicles of Pelayo, bishop of Oviedo in the twelfth century. Pelayo was an historian, and his works include *The Book of the Testaments of Oviedo*, a collection of documents compiled in book form during the first two decades of the twelfth century, and the *Corpus Pelagianum*, another collection of histories and documents related to the first kings of Asturias. Among the other documents that mention the passage of the Sudarium to Spain is the *Codex Valenciennes 99*, a French codex that predates the works of Pelayo. Although it is impossible to date it exactly, it is illustrated with miniatures of the ninth century. The story of the chest and its relics, among them the Sudarium, was added in the eleventh century. This manuscript can be found in the Library of Valenciennes, France. Three manuscripts kept in France and Belgium also relate the history of the chest of relics, and while they are not considered to be an extremely accurate compilation of events, they coincide essentially with the other accounts. These are known as the *Valenciennes 30, Cambrai B804*, and *Bruselas II 2544*. Another is known as the Chronicle of the Monk of Silos, normally called the *Silense*, which was written by an anonymous monk of Silos around the year 1115 AD, using a source independent of that of Pelayo. The final manuscript is the *Chronicon Mundi* of Bishop Lucas of Tuy, born in born in León in the second half of the twelfth century. Although based on previous documents, the writer introduces several original dates.

Based on the accounts found in these historical documents, it is possible to reconstruct the early history of the chest of relics. The first historical mention of the relic, of course, would be that of John the Evangelist, who records that the sudarium was found in the sepulcher, not with the other linens, but in a separate place. An interesting and rather surprising thing, evidence that this sudarium mentioned by John is indeed the Sudarium of Oviedo, is found in the paraphrase of the Gospel of St. John made by Nonnus of Panopolis in Egypt, written in the first half of the fifth century. He adds a few revealing details to the evangelical account of John 20:6-7:

> *When Simon Peter arrived after him, he immediately went into the tomb. He saw the linens there together on the empty floor, and the cloth that covered his head, with a knot toward the upper back of the part that had covered the hair. In the native language of Syria it is called sudarium. It was not with the funerary linens, but was rolled up, twisted in a separate place.*

As EDICES points out in their photographic exhibition, this is surprising for two reasons. First, that Nonnus knew how the Sudarium of Jesus was used, and secondly, that he makes reference to the fact that the cloth had been knotted. This description exactly fits the final position of the sudarium according to scientists, which can be seen in their photographs reproduced in this book.

Another equally interesting testimony concerning the preservation of the Sudarium of Oviedo is that found in a manuscript known as *San Antonino Mártir*, the chronicle of the pilgrimage made to the Holy Land by an anonymous pilgrim from Piacenza, Italy, in the year 570 AD. The document mentions the existence of a cave close to the Monastery of

St. Mark, on the other side of the River Jordan, in which lived seven nuns in seven cells, who – according to what they told him – "*looked after the sudarium of Christ.*"

Two other sources affirm that it was the apostle Peter who took charge of the sudarium. The first is the life of Santa Nino of Georgia, who died in the year 338. The writer relates that Peter had hidden it, and that it was not known whether or not this place had ever been discovered. Interestingly enough, this same writer also says that the three crosses, those of Jesus and the two thieves crucified with him, were buried in the city of Jerusalem, but at that time no one knew exactly where. It is commonly believed that Helen, the mother of the Emperor Constantine, visited Palestine in the year 327 or 328, where she discovered the True Cross in a cistern. Santa Nino died in the year 338, and it is believed that the autobiography was written in the final year of the author's life. By this time the discovery of the Cross would have been known, but it is not mentioned, which may support the belief that the crosses were discovered at a later date by someone other than St. Helen[3].

The second reference to St. Peter as custodian of the sudarium is that made by Isodad of Merv[4], an oasis in what today is known as Turkmenistan[5]. Isodad wrote his *Commentaries on the Gospels* in the Syriac language around the year 850, and it is believed that this Nestorian bishop collected early Eastern traditions. In the part concerning the Gospel of John, he says:

---

[3] According to *Butler's Lives of the Saints,* the Pilgrim of Bordeaux, in 333, says nothing of the discovery, nor does Eusebius, the historian. St. Cyril, Bishop of Jerusalem, in his letter to Constantius around the year 346, expressly states that "the saving wood of the cross was found at Jerusalem in the time of Constantine," but does not mention St. Helen. The first to ascribe the discovery to the intervention of St. Helen is St. Ambrose in 395, and many others can be found around the same date or a little later. Several other writers around the same time also attribute the discovery of the True Cross to St. Helen, but St. Jerome, who lived in Bethlehem, was not among them.

[4] See Mark Guscin, "¿Quién sacó los lienzos del sepulcro?" *Del Gólgota al sepulcro: Posible reconstrucción* (Valencia: Centro Español de Sindonología, 1998).

[5] Turkmenistan is a republic in central Asia, bordering the Caspian Sea, Iran, and Afghanistan.

...but they gave the burial linens to Joseph the senator [Joseph of Arimathea], *and it was right that they be returned to him for safekeeping as he was the owner of the tomb, as it was he who brought them for the honor of Jesus. But Simon* [Peter] *took the sudarium, and it was for him a crown on his head. And every time that he laid his hands on someone, he put it on his head. He obtained much and frequent aid from it, in the same way that even today the leaders and the bishops of the Church put turbans on their heads and around the neck in place of that sudarium.*

It is quite interesting that Isodad says that Peter used the cloth in the rite known as the imposition of the hands, that with the aid of the relic he was able to obtain miraculous cures, and that later bishops wore turbans, a forerunner of the miter, in imitation of the sudarium worn by Peter. While some may not agree, it seems logical to me that the Apostle would have worn the sudarium containing the actual blood of Christ in order to obtain cures. If this cloth had originally been the turban of Jesus, as some believe, that was later used to wrap His head after death, it would also be highly symbolic to find St. Peter wearing it on his head in the early years of Christianity. Additionally, it would make sense that subsequent leaders would have copied the tradition of wearing a turban, that later evolved into the bishop's miter.

It is known that St. Paul also used the type of cloth known as the sudarium to obtain cures, because it is stated in the Bible that *"so extraordinary were the mighty deeds God accomplished at the hands of Paul that when face cloths or aprons* [sudaria] *that touched his skin were applied to the sick, their diseases left them and the evil spirits came out of them."* (Acts 19:11-12). Although these cloths were clearly not the original sudarium, it is quite possible that St. Paul is using them to cure the sick in imitation of St. Peter. If not, why didn't he simply resort to the imposition of hands? The passage seems a bit strange unless it is considered within the context of Paul using the sudarium as a symbol of the original containing the blood of Christ, in imitation of Jesus and later St. Peter curing the sick. It underscores the Christian belief in the saving power of the blood of Jesus, repeated so often in the New Testament[6]. Even today, small cloths are often blessed and used to cure the sick, quite possibly a continuation of that same tradition.

It is also significant that these early sources mention St. Peter as the first custodian of the sudarium. As we will see later, this makes perfect sense in the context of John 20, the chapter that relates the finding of the linens in the tomb by Peter and John, the beloved disciple. They discover the linens, and something about the position and condition of the cloths leads John to believe in the Resurrection. The apostles then return home, but Mary Magdalene remains behind weeping. She finally looks into the tomb and sees two angels where the body of Jesus had been. There is no mention of linens at this point. Mary truly believes that the body of Jesus has been stolen, until she turns around and sees the Savior. If the linens had still been in the tomb, why did she not come to the same conclusion as John?

Most important is the fact that all of these early references confirm the traditional belief that the Sudarium was in Jerusalem for nearly six hundred years, possibly initially used by St. Peter as a sort of healing cloth, and later hidden in a cave for protection.

Another reference given by EDICES is found in the book entitled *Arculfi relatio de locis sanctis, ab Adamanno scripta,* the historical story of a journey from France to the Holy Places by the Gallic bishop Arculf, believed to have been the bishop of Périgueux. While returning from his pilgrimage, Arculf was driven by storm to Scotland and arrived at the Hebridean island of Iona. The abbot Adamnan gave the pilgrim bishop refuge and wrote a narrative of his journey to the Holy Land, which was turned over to King Alfred of Northumberland in 698. It later came to the attention of the Venerable Bede, who included a summary of the account in his *Ecclesiastical History of the English People,* and also wrote a longer version that became a popular guidebook to the holy places during the Middle Ages. The account of Adamnan specifically mentions that one day when Arculf was in Jerusalem, the Sudarium was taken out of a sanctuary and shown to the crowds; he had even been permitted to kiss it. While there is no indication of the exact date, it can be deduced that it occurred in the seventh century or earlier, before the destruction of Jerusalem by the Persians. As Arculf

---

[6] For example see Hebrews 9:12-14 which makes an analogy between the blood of Jesus and the blood of sacrificial victims. Also 1 Peter 1:2; 1 Peter 1:19; 1 John 1:7; Revelation 1:5, 5:9, 12:11.

personally drew plans of the Church of the Holy Sepulcher, if this voyage occurred at the beginning of the century, it had to have been before it was razed to the ground in 614. Since historians now believe that the Shroud of Turin had already been in Edessa, today Sanli-Urfa in Turkey, for several centuries before Arculf's pilgrimage, his reference cannot be the result of confusion between the two cloths. Nor does he mention the presence of any image on the cloth.

Nevertheless, it is likely that this is a case of confusion of terminology. According to Thomas Wright, the pilgrimage of Arculf must have taken place in the latter part of the seventh century, around the year 679 AD. The reason is that Arculf "is made to speak of 'Majuvias, king of the Saracens[7],' as having lived in his time, and the character of the story leaves no doubt that the king referred to was Moawiyah, the first khalif of the dynasty of the of the Ommiades, who reigned from 661 to 679." Wright thus places Arculf's visit to Jerusalem not long after this khalif's death. Additionally, the description given by Arculf of the Basilica of the Holy Sepulcher does not match that of the original church constructed by the emperor Constantine, an indication that his visit took place after the church had been rebuilt on a reduced scale by the priest Modestus. A further reason is that the "sudarium" of which he speaks is reported as being 8 ft. long, shorter than the Shroud of Turin, and longer than the Sudarium of Oviedo. Kersten and Gruber believe that this cloth was most probably the one given to Charles the Great around 797. It was brought to the Abbey of St. Cornelius in Compiègne a century later, and was the destination for countless pilgrims until the French Revolution, when it was destroyed.

This "sudarium" may be the case of a second shroud, which would have been used to wrap the body of Jesus during the descent from the Cross until the final entombment. Scientists are quite certain that the Shroud of Turin could not have been used for this purpose, and it is inconceivable that the body would not have been covered. This would explain some of the confusion that still exists, such as the definition given in the *Diccionario de la Real Academia Española* for "Santo Sudario,"

---

[7] Majuvias, Saracenorum rex, qui nostra aetate fuit, judex postulatus. See Wright, *Early Travels in Palestine* (London: Henry G. Bohn, 1968): p. xiii.

a subheading under "sudario": "the sheet or linen with which Joseph of Arimathea covered the body of Jesus when he lowered him from the cross[8]." This cloth, therefore, would have also contained bloodstains, but no image.

One of the difficulties involved with the history of the cloth is that there is little written documentation of early pilgrimages to the Holy Land, and it appears that it was hidden in a location unknown to most pilgrims. The earliest existing account is that of a Christian man known only as the Pilgrim of Bordeaux, the Latin *Itinerarium Burdigalense* about a pilgrimage made in 333 AD[9]. Another is that of Egeria, who visited Jerusalem between 381 and 384 AD. The text of her travels was lost for seven hundred years, and when it was found in the nineteenth century in Italy, the only part left was the middle of the book. The only veneration of relics mentioned by Egeria in this part of the manuscript is that of the Holy Cross on Good Friday. She reports that the bishop was seated before a table on Golgotha Behind the Cross, and the Wood of the Cross and the Title were taken out of a gold and silver box and placed on the table for veneration. The bishop sat with his hands resting on either end of it and held it down, and the deacons around him kept watch. The people approached the table, stooped down over it, kissed the Wood, and moved on. The reason for the guards was that on a previous occasion one of the pilgrims "bit off a piece of the holy Wood and stole it away"[10].

It is impossible to know if other relics are mentioned in the part of the manuscript that was lost, if they were not in Jerusalem at the time, or if they were simply not being shown to the public. The "sudarium" of Arculf presumably would have been in Jerusalem in the fourth century, and this cloth is not mentioned either. Due to security reasons, evident in the terrible incident mentioned above, it is quite possible that most

---

[8] "*Sábana o lienzo con que José de Arimatea cubrió el cuerpo de Cristo cuando lo bajó de la cruz.*"

[9] See Magen Broshi, "Evidence of Earliest Christian Pilgrimage to the Holy Land Comes to Light in Holy Sepulchre Church" *Biblical Archaeology Review* (December 1977) and John Wilkinson, *Egeria's Travels* (Warminster, England: Aris & Phillips, 1999), p. 22-34.

[10] See *Egeria's Travels*, p. 155. According to Wilkinson, a "large piece of the cross was stolen by a Syrian. He took it to Apamea, where it was long venerated."

relics were never exhibited, and as we have seen in the manuscript known as *San Antonino Mártir*, it appears that the Sudarium was hidden in a cave during this early period. As was the case in Oviedo, it was sufficient for pilgrims to know that the relics were in the same location; as Ramón Cavanilles Navia-Osorio mentions in his history of the Cathedral of Oviedo, piety at that time did not demand that the faithful be able to contemplate directly the objects of their devotion. Oviedo attracted innumerable pilgrims during the Middle Ages, but the chest of relics was never opened to public view. Although Jerusalem was closed to the Jews until the Muslim conquest of the city in 638 AD, a bloodstained sudarium and a shroud with an image of Christ would have been in extreme danger due to the fact that they were prohibited by the law. In fact, Ian Wilson believes that the Shroud may have left Jerusalem immediately after the death of Jesus[11].

The subject of blood will be discussed further in the third part of this book, but I am convinced that this may be one reason for the lack of early historical references. The sacred blood of Christ, the veneration of which was repugnant to the Jews, was present on two of the most precious relics known to Christianity. If we consider the history of the sudarium in Oviedo, where due to propriety and respect it was virtually hidden from view for many centuries, a tradition that has continued to a lesser extent to the present day, it is not strange that this would also have been the case during the first centuries after the death of Jesus.

The early manuscripts mentioned all agree in the following details concerning the history of the relic and its flight to Spain: a) that the relic was present in Jerusalem until the Persian invasion in the year 614, b) that it was briefly taken in a chest along with many other relics to a

---

[11] In *The Blood and the Shroud*, Wilson hypothesizes that a "disciple of Jesus called Thaddaeus or Addai travels from Jerusalem to Edessa (today Urfa, in eastern Turkey) at the invitation of the city's ruler Abgar V, with whom Jesus had purportedly been in correspondence. All accounts describe Thaddaeus/Addai healing Abgar of a disease and converting at least a proportion of Edessan citizens to Christianity. According to some versions, however, he also brings with him a **cloth miraculously imprinted with Jesus's likeness,** which later variants will describe in Shroud-like terms as bearing the full imprint of Jesus's body. This cloth we will call '**the cloth of Edessa**'." (New York: The Free Press, 1998): p. 263.

city in the north of Africa, most probably Alexandria, which was taken by the Persians in 616, c) that it was taken by sea to Cartagena on the southeastern coast of Spain, d) that it went directly to Seville during the time of St. Isidore, e) that after the death of St. Isidore in 636, Toledo became the most important city of Christianity, and the relic was taken there where it remained for 75 years, until the Muslim invasion in 711, f) that the Christians fled to the north with the relics at the time of this invasion, hiding the chest of relics for approximately fifty years in the mountains of Asturias, among them Monsacro, and g) that the chest has been in Oviedo since the city was founded in 761. All of these facts are also supported by logic and historical circumstances, as will be discussed.

Chosroes II, sometimes written as Khosrow II Parvïs (the Victorious) was proclaimed king of Persia (Iran) in the turbulent times of 590 AD. His father, Hormizd IV, had openly insulted his general, Bahräm Chübïn, after defeat by the Byzantine army at Lazica, which led to a palace revolt culminating in the King's assassination. The new king Khosrow was forced to flee to Mesopotamia, where the Byzantine emperor Mauritius enabled him to defeat his adversary, Chübïn, who was assassinated. Mauritius was later killed by Phocas, who replaced him as emperor of Byzantium. Using this as a pretext, Khosrow launched an attack, invading Armenia and Mesopotamia, where the towns of Dara, Amida, and Edessa fell. A second invasion of Mesopotamia took place in 613, with the Persians conquering Damascus. They then proceeded to Galilee.

The Jewish population, who felt oppressed by the Byzantine rulers and who hoped to regain autonomy in their own land, joined forces with the Persian invaders. Benjamin of Tiberias, a wealthy and influential Jew, contributed funds to arm the Jewish population. In the year 614 the Persians, accompanied by Jewish warriors, advanced toward Jerusalem, which fell in the month of July. Although Khosrow was generally tolerant of Christianity, his general allowed his Jewish aides to torture thousands of Christians. As many as 90,000 Christians were killed, the Church of the Holy Sepulcher was razed to the ground, and the relic of the True Cross was seized by the Persians and carried off to their capital of Ctesiphon. The Cross, which was always spoken of as the pieces of the wood of the True Cross by the original writers, was returned years later by the Emperor Heraclius in 627, an event that brought about the institution of the feast of the Holy Cross on September 14th. Nothing is mentioned of the capture or destruction of other relics, and one can assume that they were safeguarded.

During the invasion, monks were killed or banished from Jerusalem, churches and monasteries were demolished by the Jews in retaliation for the sacking of Jewish synagogues by the Byzantines, and the assault caused many Christians to waver in their faith. Many Christian laymen and clergy, including the renowned Hermit of Sinai, a Christian monk, embraced Judaism, because the restoration of a Jewish Jerusalem appeared to them as the beginning of the end of Christianity. The account of these events appears in the five-volume *History of the Jews,* originally written in Russian by Simon Dubnov, and acclaimed as the most authoritative and reliable work of its kind. It gives the reader an idea of the seriousness of this conflict, which is only briefly mentioned in most histories.

It should be kept in mind that Jerusalem and Alexandria were two of the four major sees of Orthodox Christianity since the fourth century. Constantinople was the capital of the Byzantine Empire, dedicated as the "New Rome" by Constantine the Great in 330, and Antioch was the fourth. The fall of two of these important cities could only have been considered a very serious threat to Christianity.

The Sudarium, in its coffer along with many other relics, was safely removed from Jerusalem before its destruction, and it is believed that it was taken to Alexandria by the presbyter Philip, accompanied by many of the Christians who were fleeing from the invasion. Khosrow's armies went in the same direction, however, conquering Alexandria only two years later, in the year 616. By this time the chest of relics was traveling by sea from Alexandria to Spain, possibly stopping briefly in Carthage on the northern coast of what is today Tunisia. Dr. Villalaín Blanco has discovered that it was normal procedure for ships to carry an empty chest on board as a place to deposit corpses, because death at sea was a common occurrence at that time. The chest of relics would not have aroused the least bit of curiosity or suspicion as its presence was expected.

After its journey across the Mediterranean Sea, it is believed that the chest of relics entered Spain at Cartagena. At this time Cartagena was an extremely important metropolitan diocese of the Byzantine Empire, and maintained close relations with the other Christian-Byzantine communities, among them Jerusalem and Alexandria. The relics went directly to Seville, the religious capital of the peninsula, and were placed in the custody of St. Isidore. Politician, bibliophile, historian, theologian, doctor of the church, and the last of the Western Latin Fathers, Isidore was an impressive figure under whom Seville reached an apogee in this late Visigothic period. He had many eminent disciples, among them St. Braulio (585-651) and St. Ildephonsus, who became the bishops of Zaragoza and Toledo respectively. The fame of Isidore spread along the routes of Byzantium; he was a person held in extremely high esteem for his erudition. Isidore also spent a considerable amount of time in Toledo, having been there for at least three extensive periods of time between the years 631 and 633.

St. Ildephonsus, who had possibly been educated in Seville under Isidore, became bishop of Toledo in 657. It was previously thought that when he left for the capital of the Visigoth kingdom to assume his duties, the chest of relics possibly accompanied him, but now it is believed that the relics were taken to Toledo immediately after the death of St. Isidore. Toledo had been the site of numerous famous councils, one of the greatest being the Fourth Council of Toledo (633), headed by Isidore, which decreed union between church and state, toleration of Jews, and uniformity in the Spanish Mass. After the death of Braulio in 651, and under the direction of Ildephonsus, the city of Toledo was established as the most important Christian and intellectual center in Spain, and it is logical that Spain would seek to dignify this new metropolitan see with some relics that were considered to be the most important of Christianity. They remained in Toledo for 75 years, until the invasion of the Muslims in 711 AD, an event that provoked the flight of massive numbers of Christians toward the north of Spain.

It is thought that the chest was opened at least once during its permanence in Toledo, because in the subsequent inventory of Alfonso VI, the relics of St. Ildephonsus[12] are cited. Another reference appears to corroborate this belief because Canon VI of the Council of Braga in 675 makes a rather strange reference to a *Chest of God* that contained many relics, criticizing the fact that some bishops placed them on themselves, "*as if they were the chest of the relics.*"[13]

Due to the very real threat of the Muslim invasion of Spain at the beginning of the eighth century, the Visigoths fled in the direction of the Asturian kingdom, bringing their relics with them, but the actual route is not certain. Concerning the invasion of Spain, it is known that Musa ibn Nusayr, the Arab governor of Ifrikiya (the New Arab North Africa), sent an expedition of 1,700 men into Spain under the command of his former slave Tarik. King Roderic, who had just begun his reign in 710, was in a vulnerable position, possibly also due to controversy over the succession. It is believed that many deserted him in the course of the decisive battle in the Guadalquivir valley that ended his reign and the Visigothic kingdom. In the aftermath of the victory, Tarik immediately proceeded to Toledo, encountering no resistance *en route*. Musa then brought in a large army, either later in 711 or in 712, and took Seville. Musa and Tarik together continued the northern thrust of the conquest in 714; Musa advanced into Asturias, while Tarik conquered León and Astorga.

According to some versions, the chest was taken from Toledo to the coast, and placed in a boat that carried it to Subsalas. Another legend, which I will relate a bit later, relates that it was carried in a boat to Luarca (*Lugar del Arca*, or place of the chest). Still another version says that the chest crossed Castile, passed through Babias, stopped in Torrebario, entered through the Port of Ventana and through Quirós in Asturias. From Mt. Aramo they were probably taken to Monsacro (*monte sagrado* or sacred mountain). The *Libro Gótico, Crónica Alfonsina* and the *Silense* confirm only its continual transport through caves and churches, and the chronicle of Alfonso (1465) relates that when they arrived in the mountains of Asturias, the relics were placed on top of a mountain that they call Monsacro, ten kilometers from the present city of Oviedo. Another version confuses these relics with those brought from Jerusalem by St. Toribio in the fifth century, and says that the saint arrived in Avilés with his divine cargo, and then placed the chest of the

---

[12] The holy chasuble is said to have been given to Ildephonsus by the Virgin Mary, who said to him, "Take this gift that I bring to you from the treasury of my Son." St. Ildephonsus died in 667 AD.

[13] From the Photographic Exposition of CES in the Cathedral of Oviedo.

32

relics on the peak of a high mountain called Monsacro, inside a cave, which he barricaded with timbers and covered with earth.

The legends in favor of a route to Oviedo by sea undoubtedly originated in the medieval era when Santiago was already an important pilgrimage destination, and it is possible that they may have been attempting to reinforce the importance of the relics of Oviedo, seeking a similarity with those of Santiago that were said to have arrived by sea. It may also be a case of confusing the initial arrival of the relics at Cartagena, after having followed a maritime route from Africa, with their subsequent flight to Oviedo. Nevertheless, it is known that they were hidden, either until the founding of the city of Oviedo in 761, or until King Alfonso II the Chaste (791-842) built the *Cámara Santa* or Holy Chamber to house the relics. It is believed that this room was initially the chapel of his palace, incorporated into the Gothic cathedral that was subsequently built in the fourteenth century.

A particularly important testimony has been found which corroborates the facts concerning the flight of the coffer from Toledo, previously referred to. It is the mention made by the Moorish historian Abunbenque Mohamat Rasis in his "History and Description of Spain," finished in the year 977. He writes that "*many* [of the Christians], *having left the cities, were fleeing to the mountains of Asturias and were bringing with them whatever relics they could, or were hiding them in subterranean places.*" This reference supports the belief that the relics were hidden for a period of time in Monsacro, where it is thought that they were hidden underground in a site known as the "Well of St. Toribio."

Another interesting historical reference is contained in a letter of the Bishop Braulio of Zaragoza, in which he makes a reference to the preservation of the sepulchral linens of Christ. Braulio is a saint who was the disciple of St. Isidore. He was elected bishop in 631, and died in 651. His entire collection of letters only survives in one manuscript, number 20 of the Chapter Archives of León, a codex that was discovered in the 18th century. In letter number XLII, there is a mention of *linteamina* (linens) and *sudarium*. The text says:

> ...*but in those times, it is known that many things occurred that are not written, as for example the linens and the sudarium in which the body of the Lord was wrapped. We read that it was found, but we do not read that*

*it was preserved. Nevertheless, I do not believe that the relics would have
been disregarded, but preserved for future times.*

Braulio refers to the fact that one does not read in the Gospels that the
burial linens were preserved, but says that he believes that they would
have been safeguarded by the Apostles. Not all relics are false just
because there is no Biblical record of their existence. The Bible does not
claim to be a complete record of events. Although the relics at that time
were most probably in Seville, the contents of the chest were neither
known, nor removed for public veneration.

I would like to relate one particularly charming legend, collected
by Miguel I. Arrieta Gallastegui in his book, *Historias y leyendas de
Asturias*. It demonstrates how legends concerning the origin of
important religious objects arose from the public imagination in the
Middle Ages, seeking to give a mysterious and miraculous explanation
for their origin. Although they have no basis in fact, they are a
wonderful part of the folklore, fueled by public piety. This one is
entitled "The Wolf of the Chest."

*One no longer remembers how long ago, but it was still the village that
today we call Luarca, a small town built in the meander formed by the
mouth of a river. Its inhabitants were primarily fishermen, and lived a
more or less routine life, without great excitement or unforeseen surprises:
the tides came and went with regularity and the natives saw their lives in
somewhat the same way.*

*It is not strange then, that that afternoon everyone was wide-eyed
with amazement when they saw how a strange old sailing vessel, larger
than any of the boats that they had, and with a ton of sails of every kind,
approached the port very slowly and docked. More than one person asked
himself what the devil the guard of the watchtower was doing, because it
was certainly difficult to believe that he hadn't seen it, as large and
extravagant as this vessel was.*

*The thing is that the strange boat docked without any problem and
from it emerged an equally strange personage, arrayed with loose clothing
and an enormous turban. The people were already approaching the boat to
receive this personage of such worthy presence, although inappropriate
costume, when they were surprised, once again, when they heard him*

demand the presence of a priest. For that simple group of people, it wasn't easy to understand the sudden appearance of a strange infidel who was asking, at the very first moment of arrival, for his most faithful enemy. The priest, who was already aware of the commotion that was forming in the port, quickly came down, just as he always did when something was disturbing the local peace. He also came with a bit of fear, but appeared to be supported and safeguarded by divine authority, and discussed something with the strange visitor for a few minutes. No one knows what was said, but immediately afterward activity was seen on the loading ramp and two dark personages wearing nothing but loincloths began to disembark a great chest riveted with bright ironwork. They approached the priest, and with great respect and reverence, turned the chest over to him. After a few words of farewell the strange visitor and his dark servants returned to their vessel, and as if launched by its own power, it disappeared in the sea.

There was the chest and everyone looked at it with some apprehension, but also with a certain veneration that they were reluctant to explain. Some nearby howling awoke everyone from their stupor only to put them in another: a pack of wolves, at the front of which was the largest wolf that had ever been seen in the neighboring mountains, was approaching the port. A new fear, on that day that had been converted into one full of so many fears for everyone, did not prevent the neighbors from reacting without panic or hysteria. As if it were the air itself that ordained it, the circle of people surrounding the chest opened and they allowed the wolves to pass. With a respect that is foreign to such savage creatures, the wolves surrounded the chest and the largest of them, in an unequivocal attitude of submission, prostrated itself before the chest and venerated it.

Once the wolves had gone, the priest organized the transfer of the chest to the Basilica of San Salvador in Oviedo, where it would be kept in order to be first studied and later venerated. And in memory of that wolf who was able to recognize so much sanctity, everyone called the small town that first welcomed the chest, Lobo [wolf] del Arca, or Luarca.

The legend is typical of those created around the Holy Grail and other important religious objects and relics. It takes an historical fact, that of the arrival of the chest of relics in Oviedo, and embellishes it with symbolic events that were so characteristic of the Middle Ages, in this case, the arrival of the relics by sea, like those of Santiago, the presence of a mysterious ship, present in innumerable legends including the *Romancero*[14], and the miraculous behavior of beasts, who were able to recognize the sanctity of the contents of the coffer. Luarca, a town on the northern coastal route to Santiago, would thus become significant for the pilgrims. As another legend relates that the name was derived from "Lugar del Arca," or "place of the chest," one can assume that the stories that were being circulated did not correspond exactly.

The eleventh-century French account that can be found in the previously mentioned codex of Valenciennes is based on local traditions and contains an inventory of the chest that is preceded by an abbreviated history. According to this relation, two holy men named Julian and Seranus, who had been in Jerusalem, put various relics in a box, due to fear of the pagans. They abandoned the chest in a boat at the port of Jaffa, while they went along the coast of Africa. They later found that the boat had landed in Carthage, an ancient city in modern Tunisia. The Carthaginians brought the box to Toledo along with other relics from their churches, and after mentioning the invasion of the Muslims, the account adds that the chest was then transported to the mountain of Monsacro where they remained for fourteen years until Alfonso II, the Chaste king, built the *Cámara Santa*. It is now thought that the reason for the mention of Carthage, in place of Cartagena, can be credited to the fact that the two cities had the same name in Latin[15]. The first part of the account, which relates that the relics were abandoned in a boat that miraculously landed in a city where the locals took custody of the precious cargo, is a common occurrence in legendary material concerning relics, among them those of Santiago de Compostela and the Christ of Burgos, a crucifix venerated in its

---

[14] For example, "El conde Arnaldos" relates the arrival of a mysterious ship with sails of silk and twisted ropes made of gold. The *Romancero* is a 16th-century collection of poems that had been circulating in Spain for several centuries, many about figures of medieval Spanish history, such as King Rodrigo, defeated by the Arabs in 711, and Rodrigo Díaz de Vivar, "el Cid Campeador."

[15] *Carthago* and *Carthago Nova*, mentioned by Jorge Manuel Rodríguez of CES, in a personal interview on June 19, 2000.

cathedral.

These legends, according to Cavanilles, were developed in order to explain the history of the relics that were being venerated in Oviedo by the medieval pilgrims. Writers would record various details taken from legend, history, and local tradition, mixing them in such a way that diverse variations in the story resulted. These legends, which arose from oral tradition, should not be confused with the legitimate historical records which do indeed exist, and which have been affirmed thus far by the scientific studies. While it is not presently known the exact whereabouts of the Chest of Relics from the time it left Toledo until it became established in the Cathedral of Oviedo, we do know that it was hidden in the mountains, much like the Holy Grail of Valencia which was concealed in the Pyrenees during periods of particular danger, especially after the Muslim invasion in 711 AD. Monsacro is the one of these locations, although there may very well have been other hiding places during that fifty-year period of time.

CHAPTER TWO

THE PERMANANCE OF THE RELICS IN OVIEDO

Almost from the time of the arrival of the *Arca Santa,* or holy chest, in Oviedo, it became intimately associated with this northern city. In the early Middle Ages, the veneration of relics, particularly the remains of saints and martyrs, was a religious practice that fostered the unity of communities. In ninth-century Galicia, in the northwest corner of Spain, traditionally in the year 813 AD, a bishop claimed to have discovered the remains of St. James the Apostle, the brother of St. John, buried in a rural site. Successive churches were constructed on the spot to honor the relics, and Santiago de Compostela soon became a popular pilgrimage destination. By the twelfth century the shrine of St. James was attracting Christians from all over Europe, and its popularity and fame continues even today.

The Galicians were subject to the Asturian kings, whose realm was centered in Oviedo. There the Asturians began to build up a powerful collection of relics of their own, adding to the holy chest that had come from Jerusalem. St. Eulalia, whose body was taken from Mérida, became the patron saint. According to certain documents that exist in Spain, the primitive edifices that were the foundation for the present Cathedral of Oviedo actually predate Santiago de Compostela. The Monastery of San Vicente is recorded to have been founded on the hill of Oviedo during the reign of Fruela I (757-768), around the year 761 AD, the year when it is now believed that the chest of relics came to Oviedo. It is Alfonso II, however, during whose reign the supposed tomb of St. James the Apostle was discovered in Galicia, who is credited with moving the capital of Asturias from Pravia to Oviedo. According to the *Testament of Alfonso II,* dated the 16th of November of the year 812, conserved in the Archives of the Cathedral, the Chaste King founded the Church of San Salvador and

constructed the twelve altars dedicated to each of the Apostles. The Holy
Chamber was constructed over the Crypt of St. Leocadia[16] to house the
chest of relics, so that they would not be harmed by the humidity. It was
built in the form of a church, but without any altar because the entire
room was subsequently filled with relics, chests, boxes, and tabernacles.
In the following years, kings donated precious objects that rivaled the
relics themselves in importance. One of these, the Cross of the Angels,
can still be seen in the *Cámara Santa* of the Cathedral of Oviedo, said to
have been made by angels for King Alfonso the Chaste in the year 808,
a perfectly crafted piece of gold, inlaid with a cameo and precious stones
from the royal treasury.

The Chronicle of Don Diego Alfonso of Granada, written in 1465,
relates the legend of the origin of this famous Cross of the Angels, which
quickly became a religious and political symbol, simultaneous with the
conversion of the city of Oviedo into the ruling capital of the Asturian
kingdom. The Chronicle states that King Alfonso had the main altar of
the cathedral placed in the center, and six altars to the right and another
six to the left, each one dedicated to an apostle. Later he made the
chapel of Holy Mary of the Chaste King, where his body is buried along
with some other Catholic kings, and finally the Chapel of the Angels, in
which the holy relics and the chest are now. It then narrates the miracle
of the Holy Cross of the Angels, which later led to the establishment of
September 14th, the feast of the Holy Cross, as a day of indulgences for
the Cathedral of Oviedo:

> *And this king Don Alfonso the Chaste desired so greatly to dignify this*
> *cathedral church of San Salvador of Oviedo, that one day, at the end of the*
> *Mass, ordered to be brought before him the gold and precious stones that he*
> *had in his possession. He imagined commanding that a cross be made of*
> *them, the most beautiful possible, in order to honor the church. Being in this*
> *thought, two angels in the form of pilgrims appeared before him and told*
> *him that they would make the cross that his will desired. The king hesitated*

---

[16] According to *Butler's Lives of the Saints*, St. Leocadia was a noble maiden of Toledo, who was
tortured during the persecution of Diocletian and succumbed to her sufferings in prison in
around 304 AD.

giving them his gold and precious stones, because he did not know them, but he ordered that they be given a clean room that was closed off, and went away to eat. And while he was at the table, he sent his messenger to find out what the gold workers were doing, and to give them something to eat. When the messenger of the king arrived at the door of the room, he saw such a great brightness inside that his eyes could not tolerate it, and perceived a sweet smell, as if every good spice were inside. He returned to the king, very frightened, and told him of it. The king arose from the table and went there with the prelates and rich men who were there, and when he arrived at the room he saw the same thing, the very great brightness and the very sweet smell that emanated from inside the room. Then, entrusting himself to God, with tears and devotion, he entered and found the cross already made, but did not see the masters. Then he took it in his arms with great devotion and reverence and offered it on top of the altar of San Salvador. And in this way that you have just heard this Holy Cross of the Angels was made[17].

Several other valuable religious objects were also added to the Holy Chamber during this early period. The Cross of Victory[18] was offered by Alfonso III the Great in 908, and the Agate Box[19] by Fruela II and his wife Nunilo in 910. The Cross of the Angels and the Cross of Victory are now part of the coat of arms of Oviedo and the flag of the Principality of Asturias.

Nevertheless, it is possible that these first kings didn't even get to know the contents of the chest, since, in order to avoid any possible profanity, people were made to believe that he who tried to open it would be struck down. Reminiscent of the events in the famous film *Raiders of the Lost Ark,* an historical reference from the year 1075 relates that Bishop Ponce tried to discover the contents in the year 1030. At that

---

[17] See Gallastegui, *Historias y leyendas de Asturias* (Gijón: Cimadevilla, 1998).

[18] The Cross of Victory is a Latin cross made of gold and precious stones that was ordered to be constructed by Alfonso III and donated to the cathedral in 908, exactly one century after the Cross of the Angels was donated by Alfonso II. It supposedly encloses the original oak cross that Don Pelayo raised in victory at Covadonga, site of the defeat of the Moors and the beginning of the Christian Reconquest of Spain.

[19] A reliquary box of cypress, covered with gold and precious stones.

time the chest of relics had been in the Church of San Salvador for more than two hundred years without anyone knowing exactly what it contained. One day the bishop brought together in the Holy Chamber dignitaries of the Chapter of the Cathedral, relatives, and close friends, and proceeded to open the reliquary coffer. With the lid barely raised, a "cutting and blinding whiteness" escaped from it, which frightened all those present and blinded several people, including the bishop; some of them never regained their sight.

In spite of this terrible precedent, some years later, in the year 1075, King Alfonso VI undertook a trip from Toledo to Oviedo, in order to get to know the great secret of the chest, whose fame transcended the Christian kingdom. His sister Doña Urraca accompanied him, as well as the Infanta Doña Elvira, several bishops, and Rodrigo Díaz de Vivar, *el Cid Campeador*.[20] They left during the first days of January through Pajares, arriving in Oviedo on the second of February. As the memory of the first attempt to open the coffer was still very much alive, the king ordered the celebration of services, extraordinary fasts and songs, with censors that impregnated every corner with the fragrance of incense. Filled with great fear, on March 13, on the fourth Friday of Lent, the opening of the coffer was carried out in front of the king, his followers, and the high ecclesiastical dignitaries. All were filled with amazement and gratitude to God at the sight of the incredible treasure: relics of the Passion of Jesus, of the wood of the Cross, of the Sacred Blood and of His Sudarium, as well as innumerable remains of the Holy Saints, Prophets, Martyrs, Confessors, and Virgins.

On that occasion there was no supernatural event, but there was indeed something extraordinary that occurred, according to what Jorge-Manuel Rodríguez Almenar relates in *Hallazgos Recientes*. The next day the act of the opening was recorded, and the Sudarium was incorporated definitely into the history of Asturias. In this document, the king, after a brief enumeration of the relics, made a perpetual donation of the lands of Lagneo (Langreo) to the church of Oviedo, ordered the Holy Chamber to be decorated with the famous Romanesque apostolate, and

---

[20] A military leader who became a Spanish national hero, popularized in the epic poem, *Cantar de Mio Cid*, written around 1140, according to Menéndez Pidal.

commanded that the coffer be covered with silver in accordance with its holy contents. The silver plating was carried out by an artist from Córdoba, with details done in the Mozarabic style and a splendid cover of embossed silver. The inscription on the cover not only enumerates the principal relics inside, but also clearly shows the date of 1113. It is the same chest that can be admired in the cathedral today, restored after the destruction of the *Cámara Santa* in 1934. The plating states clearly in Latin: "DE SEPULCRO DNICO EIUS ADQUE SUDARIO ET CRUORE SCISIMO," "Of the Sepulcher of the Lord and of His Sudarium and of His Most Holy Blood."

In the previously mentioned Chronicle of Diego Alfonso of Granada, diocesan judge, official, and vicar general of the diocese of Oviedo and Ruy García de Prendes, dean of the cathedral, written on Friday, June of 1465, in Oviedo, the relics contained in the chest and in the Holy Chamber are enumerated, a list that is quite impressive. It is certain that all did not come in the chest, but most likely had been collected little by little by the Asturian kings, in order to convert Oviedo and its cathedral into a place of pilgrimage, which it really came to be from the eleventh century on. While none of these have been studied by scientists as has the Sudarium, they arrived as what tradition had always maintained that they were, and have always been safeguarded and venerated as such.

The relics enumerated in the 1465 Chronicle of Don Diego de Granada[21] are indeed plentiful. In the chest itself could be found, among other items, a piece of the True Cross of Our Lord, a small stone of the sepulcher in which He was buried, some of the cloths in which He was wrapped in the manger, several thorns from the Crucifixion, a piece of the earth of Mt. Olivet touched by His feet when He ascended into Heaven, one of the thirty coins given to Judas, the chasuble given by the Virgin Mary to St. Ildephonsus, archbishop of Toledo[22], a chest of gold

---

[21] See Gallastegui, *Historias y leyendas de Asturias* (Gijón: Cimadevilla, 1998).

[22] The literary work of St. Ildephonsus includes *De virginitate perpetua sanctae Mariae*, which enthusiastically gives praise to the Virgin Mary. According to legend, our Lady showed her gratitude to the saint by appearing to him in person and presenting him with a chasuble from the treasures of her Son; this legend was immensely popular in the twelfth and thirteenth centuries.

and precious stones containing the forehead of St. John the Baptist and his hair, the hands of St. Stephen, the first martyr[23], some of the hair of St. Mary Magdalene, the sandal of St. Peter the Apostle, a sandal of St. Andrew the Apostle, the bones of many prophets and saints, relics of the holy martyrs St. Justus and St. Pastor[24], the vestment of St. John the apostle, and the ashes of St. Emilian[25], deacon. In the chapel of the Angels are the bodies of St. Eulogius and St. Lucrecia[26], martyred in Córdoba by the Moors, the body of St. Vincent, abbot of San Clodio de León, and the body of St. Olalla [Eulalia][27] of Mérida, virgin and martyr. In other parts of the Cathedral are the relics of many other saints, kings, and martyrs, as well as one of the six jugs in which Jesus made the water turn to wine, said to have been brought to the church by St. Toribio by way of the port of Avilés. It is quite evident that the wine vessel was not taken to the Cathedral by St. Toribio, who lived in the fifth century, long

---

[23] Manzano Martín relates that Avito of Braga, who helped Paulo Orosio in the Council of Jerusalem against Palagius and encouraged the presbyter Luciano so that other churches might participate in the finding of the body of St. Stephen, the first martyr, availed himself of Orosio in order to bring the relics of the saint to his Bishop Balconio, according to a letter he wrote to him. Fr. Manzano believes that the hands of St. Stephen, mentioned in the summary of the relics, may be related to the gift of Avito to his bishop during the year 415. See "Sobre los traslados del arca de las reliquias: Observaciones cronológicas" *LINTEUM* 19 (1996): 8.

[24] Two brothers, thirteen and nine years old, who, after professing their faith, were whipped and then beheaded in 304, during the reign of Dacian, governor of Spain under Diocletian and Maximian.

[25] A famous early saint and patron of Spain who lived as a hermit in the mountains above Burgos for forty years until the Bishop of Tarazona insisted that he become a parish priest. He later returned to a contemplative life and died in 574.

[26] Martyred in 850 after the Moors started a sudden persecution of Christians in Córdoba. Eulogius was a priest who, while in prison, wrote three volumes on martyrdom during the persecution and who openly proclaimed that Mohammed was an impostor. Lucretia was a converted Moslem whose parents beat her in order to induce her to apostatize.

[27] The most celebrated virgin martyr of Spain, of whom St. Prudentius wrote a hymn in her honor. At twelve years of age she presented herself before Dacian and reproached him for compelling the people to renounce their faith. After her cruel martyrdom in 304, a dove seemed to fly out of her mouth and the executioners fled in fear.

before the Cathedral was built, but was rather one of those relics that was most likely hidden at Monsacro, along with the *Arca Santa* of Oviedo.

After the solemn declaration of the relics contained in the Holy Chamber by Alfonso VI, its fame increased greatly, converting Oviedo into a major pilgrimage destination for pilgrims on the route to Santiago. Nevertheless, although a few of the relics remained outside of the chest, most were enclosed within the coffer, and pilgrims had to content themselves with touching and kissing the exterior. The fact that some of the relics were exposed presented a certain danger, however, because an anonymous author of the twelfth century relates that the wife of Alfonso (the Good and conqueror of Toledo) and a sister of hers, on the occasion of a visit to the *Arca Santa,* tried to get too close to the little boxes that were kept outside of the chest and that contained many relics. The abbot, fearful that they might take one of them, closed one of the boxes, and no one ever again attempted to open it.

After Alfonso VI ordered the opening of the chest in 1075, it remained closed for many centuries. Alfonso XI was not permitted to see them, in spite of the fact that he came to Oviedo as a pilgrim in 1345 and gave expensive gifts[28] to the Church, having to content himself with seeing only the reliquary. In fact, no one knows of anyone who might have wanted to open the *Arca Santa* until the pontificate of Don Cristóbal de Rojas y Sandoval (1547-56). According to Ambrosio de Morales, three days before the day it was to be carried out, the bishop ordered everyone to fast with prayers to Our Lord and processions. On Sunday he celebrated Mass and then went up to the Holy Chamber; there he prayed again, and on his knees in front of the Chest he took the key to open it. As he put it into the lock, however, he felt so faint that it was impossible for him to move. There remained no other choice but to refrain from opening the coffer; it even seemed to him that his hair was standing on end and that the miter was falling from his head. Morales concludes that the chest remained closed, and would remain closed for many more years due to the veneration, respect, and fear of the clergy.

---

[28] These included some goblets, a golden chalice, an enameled cross made of gold, two silver lamps, expensive ecclesiastical vestments, and a substantial donation.

It is thought by some that the chest may have been opened privately on the occasion of the consecration of Bishop Don Pedro Junco de Posada for the diocese of Salamanca, in the time of the Bishop of Oviedo, Don Diego Aponte de Quiñones (1585-1598). Cavanilles, however, doubts that this opening ever took place. On another occasion Don Juan F. de Torres, the Bishop of Oviedo, shortly after arriving in the capital in December of 1715, proposed to the Chapter of the Cathedral that the chest be opened and the relics taken out. After considering this very serious proposal and celebrating the Mass of the Holy Spirit in order to obtain divine enlightenment, they denied the petition of the prelate.

The desire to hide the relics from the eyes of the curious thus remained for many centuries, but this situation changed at some point shortly after the petition of the bishop was denied in the year 1715. Ambrosio de Morales visited the Holy Chamber, an event that was recorded in Madrid in 1765 by Antonio Marín. Commissioned by Philip II to inventory the relics of the Cathedral of Oviedo, he was permitted to see the Sudarium, and his description, which appears in the Introduction to this book, demonstrates how difficult it is to discern exactly what the Sudarium is. His general reaction was that "of these relics there is no more testimony than their tradition and antiquity," and he was particularly impressed by the notable devotion for them that "enraptures even a sinner like me." He must have felt an immense pleasure discovering the contents of the innumerable chests and boxes kept in the Holy Chamber during this conflictive period of the Reform.

It is not only the kings and bishops who were interested in the reliquary chest of San Salvador; in spite of the fact that the relics were completely hidden for so many centuries and that access to Oviedo was difficult, popular devotion grew steadily from the ninth century on, and Oviedo was converted into a popular pilgrimage destination. The pilgrims who came to Santiago de Compostela coined the expression:

Quien va a Santiago y no a San Salvador,
sirve al criado y deja al Señor.

(He who goes to Santiago and not to San Salvador,
honors the servant and forsakes the Lord.)

San Salvador is the name of the Cathedral of Oviedo, which is appropriately named for the Savior, Jesus of Nazareth. With this refrain the Asturians wished to make it known that the pilgrims who visited the remains of St. James in Santiago de Compostela and not the relic of Jesus, in Oviedo, served the Apostle instead of the Lord. It also existed with several variations, sometimes substituting *Señor* with the word *Criador* (the Creator), and the verb *sirve* with *visita* (visits). The saying was also popular in Italy and France[29].

Oviedo was not on the traditional route to Santiago, but it was so well known that many pilgrims felt that it was worthwhile to make a detour in order to visit the relics of the Holy Chamber, in spite of the difficulties involved in crossing the mountains between Asturias and Castile. One pilgrim, referring to the poor state of the roads in this part of Spain, remarked in 1501 that many pilgrims fear to stop to Oviedo on their way to Santiago, because this deviation is poorly populated, sterile, and much more mountainous that the principal route. Nevertheless, multitudes came to the Cathedral because of its treasures, and many even attempted the difficult climb to the summit of Monsacro.

Besides the fame of the relics due to the opening of the chest in the year 1075, one additional event served to attract pilgrims. This was the miracle of the expulsion of the demon that had possessed a young pilgrim woman, related in several ancient manuscripts[30] from the end of the twelfth century or beginning of the thirteenth. The description is so

---

[29] See Luciano Castañón, *Refranero asturiano* (Oviedo, 1962). According to Castañón, the article "Las peregrinaciones a Santiago de Compostela" [M. 1949, Vázquez de Parga, Lacarra, y Uría] relates that in August of 1539 the Italian pilgrim Bartolomeo Fontana said when he arrived in León: "*Qui mi disposi andar a visitar lo santo Saluator, perche so gliono dire li Peregrini, che chi va a s. Giacobo, e non a Saluatore, uisita al seruo, e lascia il signore.*" The French refrain is as follows: "*Qui a esté a Sainct Jaques et n a esté a Saint Salvateur, a visité le Serviteur et a laisse le Seigneur.*"

[30] This account is included in the manuscripts published for the first time by Ch. Köhler. Juan Uría summaries this narration in *Las peregrinaciones*, t. I, p. 431-435, and also in an article, *Una peregrina endemoniada en la iglesia de San Salvador de Oviedo*, published in "Asturias Semanal," July 19, 1969, now published in the volume *Los vaqueiros de alzada y otros estudios* (Oviedo, 1976).

vivid and full of details that, according to Cavanilles, it must have been written by an eyewitness of the events. According to this story, a woman who was impregnated against her will cursed her offspring at the moment of conception and commended the child to the devil. She cared for her daughter for seven months after birth, when the infant was carried off by the devil, and given a life of riches, servants, and attention. At the age of sixteen, the girl, although quite thin, was strong and able to speak many languages. At seventeen she was taken to an abbey of Benedictine monks in Jaca, in Aragón, where Santiago appeared to her, imprinting the sign of the cross on her finger. The devil returned, and speaking through her in terrible voices, said that he would leave her only if San Salvador or Santiago ordered it. The girl was therefore sent on a pilgrimage to the Cathedral of San Salvador where she knelt before the Holy Chest of relics. At that moment the devil once again entered her body, and began to speak. The clergy ordered the devil to leave, but he refused, explaining that he had raised the child and instructed her in all of his arts. When the archdeacon brought before the young woman the Cross of the Angels, the devil was forced to leave; the following day, however, when the girl returned to the church, the devil once again entered her. The canon, who feared that, because of the sins of the people, God might allow the devil to demolish the church, ordered that the relics be brought to him. The devil immediately left. On the third day, the girl was brought before the altar of San Salvador. The devil reentered the body and, raising her above the altar, threw her to the pavement, shouting that he would not let her go. Those in the church tried to subject her, but she was once again raised in the air. The archdeacon ordered everyone in the church to pray, and the girl was again thrown to the floor. The canon then brought the Cross of the Angels, and after a terrible confrontation, the demon finally left never to return, saying that the Savior had sent him as an example for the world. The girl remained in Oviedo for six weeks, was baptized and given the name of María; she became an extremely beautiful and charming young woman who spoke to pilgrims about the events that had transpired.

CHAPTER THREE

THE BENEDICTION AND INDULGENCES

F rom the Middle Ages on, the Holy Chamber of the Cathedral of Oviedo thus became an important pilgrimage destination for Christians, who hoped to receive indulgences and blessings by venerating its treasury, a veritable plethora of relics of every kind. Indulgences and the veneration of relics grew in importance, and were officially sanctioned in 1343 by Pope Clement VI when he proclaimed that the members of the Church could draw on the merits of Christ and the saints for the remission of the temporal punishment due to their sins. The Tridentine[31] profession of faith, formulated in the sixteenth century, thus proclaims:

> *I firmly believe that purgatory exists and that the souls detained there are aided through the help of the faithful; also, that the Saints who reign with Christ must be venerated and invoked, and that they offer their prayers to God for us, and that their relics must be venerated. I firmly affirm that the images of Christ and of the ever Virgin Mother of God, just as those of the other Saints, must be kept and preserved and given due honor and veneration; I declare that the authority of the indulgences was left to the Church by Christ, and that the use of them is exceedingly beneficial for the Christian people.*

---

[31] Formulated at the Council of Trent, which opened on December 13, 1545 under Pope Paul II. Its most important accomplishment was the reform of the Mass, which had become a "theatrical-type spectacle" during the Middle Ages. The Tridentine Mass was effective in securing a uniform religious expression for Catholics throughout the world. See Thomas Bokenkotter, *A Concise History of the Catholic Church* (New York: Doubleday, 1990): 217.

The Cathedral of Oviedo has a long tradition of indulgences, dating back to Alfonso II the Chaste, associated with the veneration of the relics contained in the Holy Chamber. Richard Ford, a 19th century Englishman who wrote a three-volume guidebook to Spain in 1845, gives an interesting account of his visit to the cathedral in the first half of the century:

> *These relics are in the* Camara Santa, *or the primitive chapel (repainted, alas!) of* San Miguel, *which is thought to be the second oldest Christian building after the Moorish invasion. It is concealed, for greater security, between the cathedral and its cloisters, and is elevated to preserve the relics from damp: 22 steps ascend to an anteroom with groined roof. Observe the arched ways, with foliage and quaint sculpture, which leads to the chapel, 26 ft. by 16. At the end, and two steps lower, is the inner sanctum sanctorum: 12 statues of the apostles, coeval with the building, support the roof, and the mosaic pavement resembles those of Italy of the ninth century, and especially the Norman-Byzantine works in Calabria and Sicily. It was once lighted up by magnificent silver lamps, which were carried off by the French. The devout kneel before a railing while the holy relics are exhibited. Morales thus writes his official report to Philip II.:—"*Estoy escribiendo en la iglesia antes de la reja, y Dios sabe que estoy fuera de mi de temor y reverencia." *such was the fear and reverence of this learned man, who trembled before these gold enshrined objects . . .*

Ford then goes on to relate his impression of the relics and the exposition of the cloth, demonstrating his rather skeptical view:

> *The Oviedo* Arca, *or chest, is really genuine, and it is made of oak, covered with thin silver plating, with* bassi relievi *of sacred subjects, and a Latin inscription round the border, which refers to the contents. Observe particularly the crucifix made by Nicodemus; it is of ivory, about a foot high: the figure exactly resembles the* Cristo de las batallas *of the Cid at Salamanca, which thus fixes its age about the 11th century. The feet are separate, and not nailed one on the other; and as this was made by Nicodemus beyond all question, it is referred to by Spanish theologians as settling a position much questioned. Here is the sandal of St. Peter, and some of the Virgin's milk in a metal box. In another small case is kept the*

santo sudario, or shroud of our Saviour, which is exhibited publicly three times a year, and always on Good Friday, when the bishop preaches: it is then displayed from a balcony which has been barbarously cut out of the staircase of the Camara Santa *in 1732. The peasants hold up loaves, beads, and other objects, which they are taught and believe do thus acquire a nutritious and medicinal quality.*[32]

The balcony mentioned by Ford was the traditional location for the benediction, now given from the main altar of the cathedral.

The *Cámara Santa,* dedicated when it was built by Alfonso II to St. Michael the Archangel, has unfortunately suffered several tragedies. It was almost completely destroyed in an explosion in the early morning of the 12th of October, 1934, from dynamite that had been placed in the crypt of St. Leocadia[33]. The Cross of the Angels and the cover of the Holy Chest were discovered near the altar in the same chapel. The seriousness of the disaster represents one of the worst in the history of Asturias, especially in terms of artistic, historical, and social repercussions. Restoration was begun in 1939, and on September 17, 1942, General Franco placed the last stone in the vault of the crypt of St. Leocadia. Many of the original works of art have been restored, particularly the Cross of the Angels and the Cross of Victory, which were found buried in the rubble, without serious damage. The Sudarium was unharmed. On another occasion, during the night of December 9, 1977, a Portuguese thief penetrated the sanctity of the inner sanctuary in order to rob the Holy Chamber of its most valuable treasures, destroying many of the objects in the process. Nevertheless, the treasury still contains an outstanding collection of ancient pieces, including the restored Cross of Victory, Cross of the Angels, Agate Reliquary, and Holy Chest.

The visitor is allowed access to the sanctuary only in the company of a guide from the cathedral, and the objects can be viewed through the iron grille that protects them. The Sudarium is kept in its silver-plated

---

[32] See *A Hand-Book for Travellers in Spain, and Readers at Home,* 1845. Vol. III, published by Southern Illinois University Press, Carbondale, Illinois, 1966.

[33] See also "Spanish Civil War" in the Glossary of this book for a more detailed account of the destruction of the *Cámara Santa.*

chest, removed only three times a year for a public benediction during the Mass celebrated on the main altar of the cathedral. These days are the same as they have been for centuries: the 14th of September, the feast of the Holy Cross; the 21st of September, the feast of St. Matthew; and Good Friday. The two dates in September are the first and last days of the Jubilee of the Holy Cross, and a plenary indulgence is granted on these occasions for those who fulfill the necessary conditions, which include reception of the sacraments of Reconciliation and Eucharist. No one holds up bread and other objects these days in the belief that they will be blessed, but on the occasion when I was present, the 14th of September, the cathedral was filled with pilgrims and visitors. A woman employed in the *Cámara Santa* informed me that most of the foreign visitors are from Italy, possibly due to the recent scientific investigations that have established a connection between the Sudarium of Oviedo and the Shroud of Turin.

The practice of giving indulgences to those who would visit the Cathedral in order to venerate the relics began during the reign of King Alfonso II the Chaste, who obtained from the Holy Father "indulgence and pardon from the third part of their sins" for all pilgrims who came to the Cathedral of San Salvador. With the surprising growth of the number of pilgrims in Oviedo, the Chapter members petitioned Pope Eugenio IV for the grace of a Jubilee that would be suitable to the antiquity, nobility, and importance of the Cathedral and of the Treasure that was being venerated there, and that also would be able to help economically solve the problem of the upkeep of the Cathedral. In the papal bull of November 10, 1438, a plenary indulgence was conceded to those who would visit the Cathedral of Oviedo on the day of the Exaltation of the Holy Cross or during the eight days before or after, during the year in which such feast would occur on Friday, and who would offer alms for the building fund of the Cathedral. The grace of the Jubilee was tied to the feast of the Exaltation of the Holy Cross on September 14th, due to the fact that the Cathedral had in its possession the Cross of the Angels, *"que opere angelico fabricata dicitur,"* in the words of the bull.

At the request of the Kings of Spain "who profess so much affection for that Cathedral Church of Oviedo," Pope Pius IV, through his Bull of November 13, 1561, extended the concessions magnanimously.

Consequently, for four entire centuries, the Jubilee would always begin on the sixth day of September and would last until the 22nd of the same month. In the years in which the feast of the Exaltation of the Holy Cross would occur on Friday, the Jubilee would begin the 14th of August and end on October 14th. In 1967, however, the Apostolic Constitution *Indulgentiarum Doctrina* of Pope Paul VI, (January 1, 1967), reordered the discipline concerning indulgences, suppressing all of those that had not been expressly recognized by the Holy Apostolic Penitentiary. This same year the Holy Penitentiary conceded *in perpetuum* a plenary indulgence only on the feast of the Exaltation of the Holy Cross to those who would visit the Cathedral Church of Oviedo and comply with the other customary conditions. The following year another plenary indulgence was established on the 21st of September, the feast of St. Matthew, and in 1982 the grace of plenary indulgence was conceded during the entire eight days from the 14th to the 21st of September. This practice is being observed since then: the possibility of attaining plenary indulgence on all of the days belonging to the Jubilee of the Holy Cross, between the 14th and the 21st of September.

A Jubilee, then, is a solemn plenary indulgence granted by the Holy Father, which is the remission before God of the temporal pain due to the sins whose guilt has already been pardoned. The theology of indulgences is based upon the concept that even though a crime and the eternal punishment are forgiven in the sacrament of Reconciliation, God's justice demands that the sinner pay for his crime, either in this life or in purgatory. Indulgences may be either plenary, the remission of all temporal punishment due to sin, or partial. They may also be applied to the souls of the dead, in the manner of aid or suffrage. The conditions in order to receive the plenary indulgence during the Jubilee of the Holy Cross are these: a) A pious visit to the Cathedral of Oviedo and praying the Our Father and Creed, b) the sacrament of Reconciliation, c) receiving the Eucharist, and d) prayer for the intentions of the Holy Father (Our Father and Hail Mary, or other pious prayer).

Pope John Paul II himself has visited the Holy Chamber of the Cathedral of Oviedo, where he venerated the relics of the martyrs that are kept in the *Arca Santa*. Later he contemplated the Cross of the Angels and the Holy Sudarium.

CHAPTER FOUR

MONSACRO AND THE RELICS OF ST. TORIBIO

The final subject that I would like to address in this part of the book is Monsacro, the nearby mountain where the chest of relics is believed to have been hidden until the danger of the Arab invasion had passed. This mountain, whose peak rises about 1,057 meters, is situated to the south of the city of Oviedo between two rivers, the Nalón and the Riosa. Many of the pilgrims who came to Oviedo to see the relics on their way to Santiago de Compostela traditionally attempted to climb to the top in order to visit the well of St. Toribio, located in the interior of the octagonal chapel of the ancient Church of Our Lady of Monsagro, pray on the sacred summit, and collect thistles and earth as miraculous souvenirs. It was quite a feat, as winter snows, spring mire, and autumn rains impede access to the chapel for most of the year. For this reason, knowledge of its existence, outside of the Principality of Asturias, has not been well known. There are two hermitages, but the chapel on the summit is that of Our Lady of Monsagro, a Romanesque building whose construction was carried out in four phases. The oldest part is the octagonal nave which conserves a hollow altar that covers a well with a depth of about one meter, the "Pozo de Santo Toribio," which some believe is the funerary room of a dolmen or ancient burial mound. The name of the mountain originated in the time of the cult to Jupiter, to whom almost all of the sacred mountains were dedicated, such as Montem Sacrum, Monte Sagrado, and Monsacro. The statue of a Black Madonna was venerated there as Our Lady of Monsagro, an image that disappeared during the Spanish Civil War.

According to Rafael Alarcón, there are two versions of how the relics arrived in the mountains of Monsacro where they were hidden in a cave. The first relates that St. Toribio of Astorga, a bishop sometimes erroneously called St. Toribio of Liébana, a monk who lived at the same time, made a pilgrimage to Jerusalem in the fifth century. Under the threat of a Persian invasion and after experiencing a dream in which he was warned to remove as many relics of the Passion as possible from the Holy Places, made two groups and placed them in small boxes, which were then deposited in a fine chest. After arriving at the Asturian coast, he made the journey to Monsacro and ascended the mountain with his divine treasure; as the chest was quite heavy, he stopped to rest on a projecting rock, still known as the "bishop's seat." Once at the summit, he deposited the chest in the interior of a dolmen, which became known later as the "Pozo de Santo Toribio." St. Toribio later undertook the construction of an hermitage over the well, dedicated to Our Lady, and enthroned in it an image of the Virgin that he had brought from Jerusalem, said to have been carved by St. Luke, the Evangelist.

The other version is that which I have already related. Alarcón suggests that the most likely solution would be that the relics brought by St. Toribio, Bishop of Astorga, in the fifth century preceded the chest now found in Oviedo, which came from Toledo in the eighth century. Both collections were hidden together on Monsacro until Alfonso II transferred them to Oviedo. The relics of St. Toribio are now safeguarded in the Monastery of St. Toribio of Liébana, formerly called the Monastery of St. Martin. The most important of these relics is the largest fragment of the True Cross in the world, a piece of the left arm that contains the original nail hole, kept in a reliquary in the church and displayed for public veneration. It is not known, however, exactly when the relics arrived in Liébana, but it is thought that the body of St. Toribio and his relics were placed in the monastery at the end of the ninth century, although an inventory was not carried out until the fourteenth century. This date supports the hypothesis that the two groups of relics were together for some time.

There is, however, another possibility. A third hypothesis would be that all of the relics of Monsacro either came with the original chest which arrived in Cartagena after the Persian invasion of 614, or were added to these relics during the subsequent one or two hundred years. There is evidence that would lead one to believe that, although St. Toribio of Astorga is a real saint, the story of the relics he brought from Jerusalem is purely legendary, perhaps developed in the years when

Oviedo was becoming known as a pilgrimage destination. Because the veneration of relics was so important in fostering the self-consciousness of communities, it is quite possible that some of the relics that were originally in Oviedo were taken to Liébana, where they took on an identity of their own.

An interesting and confusing coincidence is that the inventories of both groups of relics have several items in common. The list of the relics of Oviedo mentions a large fragment of the True Cross, and that of Liébana in 1316 lists a *"gran parte del Sudario de Christo."* To my knowledge, Oviedo does not display a fragment of the True Cross, and the Monastery of Liébana does not expose for public veneration any other relics it may have in its possession. One would think that if the monastery really believed it possessed a relic as important as the Sudarium of Christ, a cult would have developed over the years as it did in Oviedo.

Furthermore, it is most interesting that nearly all of the relics of St. Toribio also appear in the inventory of Oviedo. Most are fairly insignificant – such as bread from the Last Supper, a stone from the sepulcher, and earth from the Holy Land – and none of these are currently in the Monastery. The inventory of St. Toribio also repeats the story of the first opening of the chest, when the spectators were reportedly blinded, an extremely significant detail that supports the hypothesis that the relics were originally some of those from Oviedo.

A further problem is that it is quite certain that the True Cross was taken by the Persians during the invasion of Jerusalem in 614. Although it may be possible that part of the Cross was taken almost two centuries earlier by St. Toribio, why did he leave the rest of it in Jerusalem at that time? While the Persian invasion of 614 is well documented and was a serious threat to the safety of the relics, I have not been able to find a single historical reference to a Persian invasion of Jerusalem in the middle of the fifth century, another argument in favor of the theory that the relics found in Liébana are some of those that were originally in Oviedo, and that the legendary tradition of St. Toribio's pilgrimage to Jerusalem evolved over the years in homage to the saint, with details copied from the history of the *Arca Santa.*

J.M. González[34] even believes that it is possible that the "Toribio" of Monsacro comes from a linguistic phenomenon related to the ancient dolmen of the well. In Asturias the deformation would come from the pre-Roman base *taurus*, the word for diverse funerary mounds, which evolved into *turo, turelo, turumbo, torimbo* and *torimbio*. Interestingly enough, *taurus* is also the Latin word for bull, which is *toro* in Spanish. Monsacro has traditionally been used as a summer pasture for cows and bulls that cover the summit to the present day.

After formulating this thesis, I sent an email to Jorge-Manuel Rodríguez, vice-president of CES. He immediately informed me that they are in complete agreement with this theory; it is the very same idea upheld by Dr. José Delfín Villalaín Blanco, professor in the Department of Legal Medicine of the University of Valencia and vice-president of EDICES, among others.

There is other interesting material to support this hypothesis. Monsacro, according to Alarcón, was connected with religious cults long before Christianity was established in Spain. The dolmens belong to the first phase of its existence, accompanied by a cult to the Great Mother that was assimilated later to solar worship. With the arrival of the Romans, almost all of the sacred mountains were dedicated to Jupiter. When the Council of Toledo in 681 and 682, as well as the Council of Rouen of 698, condemned the cult to the dolmens, it was substituted with the "well" of St. Toribio. The cult to the Great Mother Earth was replaced with the veneration of the Black Madonna, said to have been carved by St. Luke and brought from Jerusalem by St. Toribio. This Roman image unfortunately disappeared during the Spanish Civil War, but the ancient legend of the apparition of the image, the Virgin of Monsagro, seems to support this theory:

> *Finding himself at the top of the mountain pasturing his animals, a herdsman, and it is not certain if he was from Llanera or Siero, saw that the golden ox was going into the open octagonal chapel. Setting out to look for him, he found him kneeling before the altar of St. Toribio, still scratching and bellowing. The herdsman couldn't pull the animal away, and the ox persisted in doing this the entire day. As the afternoon drew to*

---

[34] See Rafael Alarcón Herrera, *A la sombra de los Templarios* (Barcelona: Martínez Roca, 1986), p. 224-240.

an end, the herdsman ran to the town with the news. The good man insisted so much that, in spite of the mistrust his type aroused in the people, some of the villagers, without waiting for morning, undertook the trip to the summit of Monsacro, accompanied by the priest. They arrived at nightfall.

To their amazement, they found the animal in the same posture, surrounded by a golden radiance. The priest, understanding this to be something divine, ordered that they remove the altar and dig in the well of the Saint. After a few mounds had been removed, a sealed box appeared, which once opened was seen to contain a precious image of the Virgin Mother, completely dark, 'as a girl coming down the side of the mountain,' with a child in her lap. They decided to place such a miraculous finding in the other chapel below, which was in good shape and capable of housing with dignity the divine image; later all returned to the town, after leaving the herdsman there to watch over it, along with other volunteers.

But when the authorities and the mob of curious people arrived the following day, after opening the doors they contemplated, aghast, the empty altar. The image had disappeared. They chastised the guardians, who ended up accusing the unfortunate herdsman of the theft, who was suspected of being a pagan, among a thousand other atrocities. He was quickly condemned to the gallows that they improvised on the closest tree. But when the unjust sentence was about to be fulfilled, from the door of the hermitage above they could hear the bellowing of the ox, once again surrounded with light; everyone ran to the octagonal chapel, went to the well, and found the box and image inside. The crude peasants still didn't understand the significance very clearly; there were those who spoke of a miracle and those who persisted in believing that the herdsman was guilty. Therefore, they decided to double the watch that night, at the same time that they put the unfortunate herdsman in a trap with 'strong iron.'

The following morning the image had disappeared once again, in spite of the fact that the herdsman was completely immobilized in his trap in the hermitage below. The peasants once again hurried to the hermitage above and the ox was already there, waiting at the door. They took a quick look at the well, and the box and Virgin were inside, which they carried once again to the chapel of the Magdalene. The nocturnal guard was redoubled, and they looked askance at the herdsman, who they were beginning to call a sorcerer.

In the face of the prevailing desperation, the watchmen were asleep at dawn, and the image and herdsman were gone. And once more the ox was bellowing from the octagonal chapel, but this time the surprise was twice as great, because the herdsman was there, shackled in his trap, and the Virgin was inside the well. They finally understood that the herdsman was innocent – they were indeed dimwitted – and all of what had happened was the way in which Our Lady of Monsagro wanted to manifest her desire that they reconstruct the chapel above and keep the image there. As it was to be expected, the herdsman remained there as a hermit of Our Lady, dying at an advanced age with fame as a holy man, which is more that one might expect from a herdsman of the Middle Ages.

As Alarcón points out, many symbols of the ancient cult to the Sun and to the Great Mother Earth appear in the legend. These cults persisted syncretized with Christianity, which he believes is always the case with the Black Madonnas that are so prevalent in Spain. In this legend the Virgin of Monsacro is found by a solar animal, a "golden" ox[35], surrounded with light, whose owner is a lowly herdsman, an outcast of society. It is evidence once again that the "Toribio" of the well may be more related to the word *taurus* with its double meaning of funerary mound and solar animal[36], symbol of the Great Mother Earth, than to the Saint of Asturias.

After reading the legend related above and making the climb to the summit of Monsacro, it is not difficult to imagine how it evolved. The two medieval hermitages are located at the summit, but the chapel of the Magdalene, located below the octagonal chapel containing the well of St.

---

[35] According to Cirlot, the ox became a symbol of sacrifice, suffering, patience and labor, and in Rome was regarded as an attribute of agriculture. Biedermann says, "Many legends feature oxen that pull a wagon containing a relic or the body of a saint only to a certain point (which later becomes a shrine for pilgrims), thus carrying out God's intentions." See Cirlot, *A Dictionary of Symbols* (New York: Barnes & Noble, 1995), p. 247-48, and Biedermann, *Dictionary of Symbolism* (New York: Meridian, 1994), p. 251.

[36] According to Becker, the bull (*toro, taurus*) is also a solar animal that symbolizes fecundity and productivity. In Egypt the god of fecundity Apis took the form of a bull, generally with the solar disc between its horns. See *Enciclopedia de los símbolos* (Barcelona: Robinbook, 1996), p. 316.

Toribio, is not as protected as the other. When my husband and I arrived at the top of the mountain, there were dozens of cows and bulls, and one particularly belligerent bull, that seemed to be guarding sacred ground, bellowed loudly whenever we approached the lower chapel. The octagonal chapel is located some distance above the first, nestled in the summit, and is traditionally considered to be more sacred because it covers the ancient well.

Pedro Alvárez, in his book *El Monasterio de Santo Toribio de Liébana y el "Lignum Crucis",* states his own opinion concerning the origin of the relics of St. Toribio. According to this Spanish author, St. Toribio of Astorga was born in the ancient province of Galicia at the beginning of the fifth century. He made a pilgrimage to Jerusalem, where the patriarch Juvenal named him custodian of the Holy Relics. According to tradition, while in Jerusalem he had a vision in which he contemplated the grave danger of the Holy Relics, due to the imminent invasion of the Persians. He returned to Spain with a large fragment of the True Cross and a chest full of relics, and died around the year 480. Alvárez believes that the relics that he brought from the Holy Land were later brought to Liébana during the Arab invasion of Astorga in 714.

It is believed that the Holy Chest of Relics containing the Sudarium of Oviedo left Toledo for Monsacro around the year 711, and it is therefore possible that the relics were hidden together for a very short time in the "Well of St. Toribio" found in the hermitage on the mountain, if Alvárez is correct in his assertion that St. Toribio's relics arrived in Liébana in 714. It is a fact, however, that the fragment of the True Cross does not appear in an inventory in Liébana until 1316 AD, and that there is no documentary evidence of its whereabouts prior to that date. In my most recent visit to the Monastery of St. Toribio in June of the year 2000, it is stated in the photographic exhibition for the Jubilee of the Cross that it generally accepted that the relics came to Liébana sometime in the ninth century, a time period that is perfectly compatible with the hypothesis that the fragment of the Cross was given to the Monastery by the Cathedral of Oviedo.

The most convincing evidence, however, is presented in Alvárez's book, which seems to contradict his own theory. According to Alvárez, after the crucifixion and death of Jesus, Palestine continued to be ruled by Rome. Calvary and the Holy Sepulcher were reduced to rubble, and the Emperor Hadrian ordered that a temple to Venus be constructed on the site in the second century. When the Emperor Constantine and his mother, Helen, were converted to Catholicism in the fourth century, Helen carried out a search for the True Cross, ordering that excavations be made on Calvary. Three crosses were found in a rock cistern just east of the site. In order to identify the True Cross, the bishop of Jerusalem, Macarius, ordered that a cadaver be placed upon each cross; when the body was touched to the True Cross, the man came back to life[37]. St. Helen then divided the Cross into three pieces: The vertical pole was divided into two parts; one was entrusted to her son, the emperor, who lived in Constantinople; the other was sent to the Pope in Rome. The horizontal crossbeam remained in Jerusalem, and the Church of the Holy Sepulcher was built to safeguard it. This crossbeam, or *patibulum*, would therefore be the part of the Cross taken by Khosroes II during his invasion in the year 614 AD, returned later by Heraclius. It is unlikely that half of it had been taken nearly two centuries earlier for no apparent reason. Furthermore, Adamnan wrote in the second half of the seventh century that Arculf saw the Cross in the Church of St. Sophia in Constantinople in three pieces: "the long timber cut in two, and the transverse part of the same holy cross.[38]" This account supports the belief that the Persians had taken the entire crossbeam, and that it was divided at some later date. Because the relics of the Cross were regarded in Constantinople as being too sacred for public exhibition, as is the case with the Sudarium today, there is little detailed information about them. Tracing the history of the fragments of the True Cross would be an occupation of formidable magnitude.

While one cannot be absolutely certain that St. Toribio of Astorga did not bring the left arm of the Cross to Spain nearly two centuries earlier, there appears to be no historical motivation for this event. A substantial fragment of the Cross is mentioned in the inventory of Oviedo, and it is unlikely that it is the question of an additional piece of

---

[37] There are other versions of this miracle, depending on the source.

[38] Thomas Wright, *Early Travels in Palestine* (New York: Ktav Pub. House, 1968), p. 12.

[39] Paul Devereux, *Secrets of Ancient and Sacred Places* (London: Blandford Press, 1992).

the cross. If the relic in Liébana is authentic, and there appears to be no evidence that it is not, it would most likely have arrived in Spain sometime in the eighth century, brought to Oviedo because this city, in its geographically protected location, had already begun to acquire fame for its collection of relics.

Although the confusion between the relics of St. Toribio and those of Oviedo remains an enigma, it is certain that Monsacro would have been a perfect place to hide relics during the Arab invasion of Spain. It was inaccessible, unknown to most of the population, and was considered to be a sacred mountain since ancient times. It might be added that some of the most sacred places in Europe, such as Chartres Cathedral in France and the Cathedral of Santiago de Compostela, are believed to have been sacred sites for centuries, perhaps for millennia. Chartres is thought to have once been a major Druidic center, originally a Neolithic mound containing a dolmen or a cave. In this cave, according to Louis Charpentier, a Black Virgin was found that was later destroyed in the French Revolution, made by Druids who prophetically carved the image of the future mother of the Savior[39]. Santiago de Compostela, on the other hand, was the end of the earth, Finisterre, with a multitude of Megalithic remains. Considered sacred for centuries, these places were converted into major pilgrimage centers after the birth of Christianity. Similarly, Monsacro was converted from an ancient druid center into a sacred mountain with great significance for Christians.

In conclusion it can be said that it appears that the relics of Liébana are unrelated to St. Toribio of Astorga. It seems to be much more likely that the famous relic of Liébana was brought to Spain at some point after the *Sudarium Domini* arrived in Oviedo, and that the legend of St. Toribio's vision in Jerusalem was the fictitious invention of the local populace, developed to give credence to the so-called "Well of St. Toribio" in the hermitage on Monsacro, as well as to create a separate identity for the Monastery of Liébana. Relics were continually added to the chest of relics of Oviedo during its permanence in Spain, and it is probable that this was the case with the fragment of the True Cross.

---

[39] Paul Devereux, *Secrets of Ancient and Sacred Places* (London: Blandford Press, 1992).

PART TWO

SCIENCE VS. RELIGION: THE SUDARIUM REVEALS ITS SECRETS

But when they came to Jesus and saw that he was already dead, they did not break his legs, but one soldier thrust his lance into his side, and immediately blood and water flowed out. An eyewitness has testified, and his testimony is true; he knows that he is speaking the truth, so that you also may [come to] believe.

JOHN 19:33-35

CHAPTER FIVE

THE SCIENTIFIC INVESTIGATION

With all the apparent confusion produced by the historical situation – the lack of documentation, legends mixed with facts, human error in record-keeping, and perhaps even deliberate falsification of manuscripts – one might wonder if it is possible to "prove" the authenticity of a relic. Those who put their faith in the existence of written records would point to these errors, contradictions, and the lack of documentation and say that no, it is not possible to trace the whereabouts of an historical object of great significance throughout history, much less prove its authenticity. There are too many variables, too many versions of the story, and not enough hard evidence. However, we are living in an age in which historical documentation is not the only means at our disposal. With the birth and development of modern science – forensics, hematology, palynology, polarized imagery, mathematics, and the computer – it is possible to reconstruct a crime, for example, and even convict a criminal, by analyzing whatever evidence is at the scene.

In fact, the process of investigation used for the study of the bloodstains of the Sudarium is the same as that employed in a criminal investigation. The analyses of EDICES were carried out in the laboratory of criminology and forensic biology, first in the School of Legal Medicine of Madrid and later in that of Valencia. The hematological study was directed by Dr. Villalaín Blanco.

In the case of the Sudarium of Oviedo, scientists have indeed been able to determine important information contained on the cloth, such as its age, the route it followed to Spain, the cause of death of the person whose face it covered, how soon after death it was applied and when it was removed, how it was wrapped on the head, the position of the deceased when it was positioned on the head, all subsequent moves of the body, foreign objects that came into contact with it, and substances that were applied to the cloth. While this may not constitute "proof" for some people in the case of a religious relic believed to contain the actual blood of Jesus of Nazareth, one must remember that this type of information is sufficient in our society to convict a murderer for life. It is hard evidence that cannot be falsified. The information contained on the cloth has accumulated from the moment it was made until the present day; it only remains to conduct a thorough analysis of every aspect of the cloth, which is precisely what the investigative team of CES is in the process of doing.

If the Oviedo cloth had been saturated with the blood of a pig, for example, it would have already been exposed as a fraud. In the unlikely event that, as some suggest, the shroud and the sudarium had been falsified by deliberately crucifying an innocent victim, the mathematical odds are astronomically small that all of the circumstances would match what we know about the death of Jesus, and that an image would have been obtained in the case of the Shroud of Turin. The two cloths could not have been falsified at the same time. How, for example, could the position of the puncture wounds on the back of the neck match on both cloths? How could the blood type, as well as every major bloodstain and every wound correspond?

On the contrary, after more than ten years of painstaking analysis by a group of about forty scientists, nothing has been found that would indicate that the Sudarium of Oviedo is not authentic. The results of every test undertaken, with the possible exception of one, carbon dating, are completely compatible with Biblical accounts of the crucifixion of Jesus of Nazareth. As EDICES expressed it, if a scientist has the results of 99 tests which are in favor of authenticity, and only one which is not, he would not throw out the 99 and accept the one, but would examine the one which is not in favor to determine the possibility of error. In the case of carbon 14 and the Shroud of Turin, this is exactly what scientists have been doing for the past 12 years, and in the process have contributed a wealth of valuable information about the testing process and the particular problems involved in determining the age of linen cloth. Nevertheless, as will be discussed later, the results of the carbon 14 testing that were supposedly carried out on the Sudarium cannot be considered as a relevant factor, due to a multitude of errors, contradictions, and doubts that it was ever performed.

While the complete record of the initial phase of scientific testing is carefully documented in the book, *Actas del I Congreso Internacional sobre el Sudario de Oviedo,* written in Spanish, this information would be meaningless to the average reader even if a copy existed in English. Therefore, I will simplify the results as much as possible, and then focus on the interpretation of the results, as well as a possible reconstruction of the events.

When the cloth is viewed by the public, it is seen sewn to a base of white tautened cloth and mounted on a stretcher, finished with a silver frame, which rests directly on the cloth without touching the relic. There is no other protection, and the linen is exposed to the elements. It was previously nailed with silver tacks, as Ambrosio Morales has indicated, that were later substituted by iron ones, which have left their oxide mark on the borders of the cloth. Normally the shorter dimensions of the rectangle are in a vertical position, with an existing seam in a torn area of the linen situated at the upper end. The side visible to the public has been called the *obverse* by the investigative team, and the side not visible, the *reverse.* Not everything is identical on both sides of the cloth. What the observer notices first on the *obverse* side are two symmetrical stains of a brown color, in various intensities. These stains also correspond with those on the reverse side, having easily penetrated the cloth. The *reverse* side has a much greater degree of contamination, and the folds of the wrinkles are clearly dirtier, an indication that this was the side traditionally exposed to the public. This is also the side that came into direct contact with the face of the crucifixion victim whose head it covered. The asymmetrical stains appear on the lower left side of this surface.

These bloodstains have a washed-out appearance, and this has been determined to be due to the fact that the stains are a mixture of blood and water, produced by the pulmonary edema that is characteristic of crucifixion victims. John mentions this in his account of the death of Jesus, that when one soldier thrust his lance into his side, "immediately blood and water flowed out." Although some may believe that this reference is purely symbolic, the blood and the water are apparent on the cloth of Oviedo, a testimony of the manner of death as well as of its reality, which refutes the heresies that deny that Jesus died on the cross. John knew nothing about pulmonary edema as the cause of death of crucifixion victims; he was only testifying to what he saw, which has been proved by science to be accurate.

Using a variety of techniques, EDICES has done a thorough textile study of the cloth. Some of these include: a) Conventional photography, which has allowed morphological studies of the stains to be carried out, as well as anthropological studies, medical-forensic studies, and detailed studies of the diverse materials adhered to the linen, b) Infrared reflection photography, to detect inscriptions or other marks hidden from the naked eye, c) Photography with ultraviolet light, to identify the different concentrations of blood and to detect substances that would otherwise remain invisible, d) Transparency photography, to study the texture and lack of uniformity of the cloth, and to help determine how the stains were formed, e) Photography with lateral illumination, to enhance the wrinkles and folds that are not noticeable with frontal illumination, and f) Electronic treatment of the image, in order to study the negative images, assign false colors to the levels of gray, and give three-dimensional effects.

Some of the most important scientific conclusions can be summarized as follows.

The morphology of the linen

As previously mentioned, the Sudarium of Oviedo is a rectangular cloth, 85.5 x 52.6 cm (about 34 x 21 inches), with irregular edges due to the handling it has received through the centuries. The cloth does not have selvages on any of its edges, or any dyes. There is a small tear, about 5.5 cm. long, in the upper right quadrant, and an oval hole is evident in the central part (12.4 x 19.6 cm).

The linen is composed of taffeta ligaments, with the threads twisted in the form of a Z, the simplest form of weave. This type of twisting is not the most common among the weaves of linen produced in the Orient before the Middle Ages, which was normally a twist in the form of an S. The Z twist was most frequently used in the weaves of the Roman Empire. Of the 33 cloths found in the caves of Qumran, only one is woven in a Z, while the rest have an S weave, but these cloths are much thicker than the Sudarium. The Oviedo cloth also has an appreciable number of defects that can be placed in three categories: loops, basting stitches due to a lack of tension, and the crossing of parallel and adjacent threads, a mistake that has been found in Danish cloths made on vertical looms with weights, from 400 BC to 500 AD. The data point to the fact that the Sudarium is an ancient linen cloth, possibly made on a vertical loom with weights. Its origin could be in the Roman Empire. The presence of other natural fibers such as cotton or wool has not been detected, nor any type of printing. It was also a fairly coarse, inexpensive cloth, unlike the linen of the Shroud of Turin, which was quite expensive.

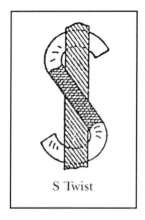
S Twist

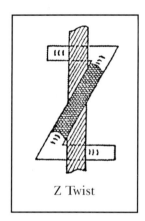
Z Twist

Pollen and other substances

Collecting samples of the dust on the cloth by means of an adjustable pump with slight suction, the palynologists of EDICES have indicated the presence, among other things, of pollen of three fundamental types: *Quercus* (oak), *Pistacia palestina* (mastic tree, terebinth tree), and *Tamarix* (tamarind tree, salt cedar), as possible geographical indicators of the presence of the Sudarium in Palestine. The other pollens that have been identified clearly indicate a flora characteristic of the Mediterranean region. A total of 141 pollens and 10 spores include such types as alder, juniper, oak, olive, pine, black poplars, sagebrush, nettle, terebinth, bramble, tamarind, salt cedar, thistle, clover, garlic, chestnut and willow. It is considered that 99% of the taxons correspond to Mediterranean vegetation, including Palestine, and 1% to Atlantic vegetation. It has therefore been concluded that the route followed by the Sudarium is clearly through the Mediterranean region, whose typical forest is composed of oak or scrub oak. The traditional odyssey of the cloth, as mentioned in the first part of the book, was first from Jerusalem to Alexandria, and then across the Mediterranean Sea to Spain, a voyage that corresponds perfectly to the pollens found on the relic.

The vegetation in Palestine is typically Mediterranean; the Palestinian thicket has the name of "batha," with the presence of the kermes oak accompanied by the terebinth tree. Certain trees and bushes, such as the pines, poplars, alders, savins and junipers, are all Mediterranean and also found in Palestine. The willows are trees and bushes typical of the corridor forests that border the rivers and are widely cultivated in gardens and used since ancient times to make different types of baskets. The chestnut belongs to the Atlantic vegetation, found in Spain in the humid northern zone. Its presence on the cloth indicates its safekeeping once in Oviedo.

The presence of aloe and myrrh has been positively identified on the cloth, as well as residues of beeswax, vegetal wax, and conifer resin. The aloe appears in greatest quantity in the areas in which there is more blood, and appears on top of this blood, which means that it was applied to the cloth after the stains were formed. Aloe and myrrh are aromatic substances that, as will be discussed later, were believed to be capable of preserving the body after death. They were used in the burial rituals of first century Palestine, and John mentions that Nicodemus brought a mixture of myrrh and aloes to the tomb to anoint Jesus (Jn 19:39). Evidence of dust from the explosion of 1934, in which the Holy Chamber was destroyed, was also positively identified. There is also a small stain from silver paint, possibly used to repair the frame at some point during the history of the cloth in Oviedo, and lipstick from a kiss given by one of the faithful.

Wrinkles

A great number of wrinkles, large and small, are noticeable on the linen, which has made this particular study quite difficult. For that reason the investigation is still open to further study. They can be generally classified in two groups: those that have the same antiquity as the stains, and those that were formed later, during the course of history. Of those that fall into the first group, several define the axis of symmetry of the bloodstains. The most notable of these is the fold between the principal stains, formed where the cloth was doubled back on itself because an obstacle prevented it from completely surrounding the head. Another prominent example is the series of diagonal folds in the upper right corner, formed when, after the head was wrapped, the remainder of the cloth was folded in this manner. Another group of wrinkles was formed when the cloth was re-wrapped to form a hood, knotted at the top of the head. By studying these wrinkles, the scientists of EDICES have been able to determine how the Sudarium of Oviedo was used.

Holes

There are several rows of holes on the cloth, produced by the sharply pointed objects that were used to fasten it to the beard and hair of the subject. They appear in a series of groups of two. Because of the conical shape of the holes, it is believed that thorns may have been used to secure the cloth, because an ordinary pin has a uniform thickness, while a thorn does not. There is another larger hole on the cloth, a burn very possibly produced from the flame of a candle, because wax has also been detected on its edges. There are also very tiny holes around the perimeter of the cloth, produced when it was sewn to a supporting cloth, and also holes from nails that were previously used to fasten it to a wooden frame.

The forensic blood analysis: the stains and their formation

The cloth, as previously mentioned, is covered with clear brown stains, of varying intensity. The stains can be divided into three groups according to their characteristics: 1) The principal stains that form two geometrical figures, 2) the stains in the shape of dots, and 3) a stain in the shape of butterfly wings, located about 10 centimeters below the previous ones. These stains have been positively identified as human blood, type AB, a mixture of one part blood and six parts pulmonary edema fluid, which is the reason for their "washed-out" appearance.

In order to study the cloth, EDICES divided each side of the linen into two "surfaces": left and right, taking as the dividing line the central fold that forms the axis of symmetry of the principal stains. There are thus four areas: right reverse, left reverse, right obverse, and left obverse. The left reverse section was in direct contact with the flow of blood from the nose and mouth; therefore, the right reverse would have been the last to have been formed. The order of formation is as follows: 1) left reverse, 2) right obverse, 3) left obverse, and 4) right reverse.

The principal stains are situated in the central area of the linen, and easily saturated all four surfaces of the linen. They are well defined, extensive, and of a darker color than the rest. These conform to the facial features of the victim, and are symmetrical because the cloth was folded back on itself as it was being wrapped around the head. Within the two groups of major stains can be seen distinct minor stains, produced after the contour stain was formed. The side that was in contact with the face of the deceased has a far greater degree of filth. This side, the *reverse*, is that which was traditionally exposed to the public, considered to be the more important side.

It was proved that in order to form these stains, the head had inclined 20 degrees to the right and 115 and 70 degrees forward, in relation to the vertical axis, and that the liquid from the pulmonary edema had to have come from the nose and mouth. This calculation demands two postures of the body: the body in a vertical position with the head inclined forward and right, and later, the body in a horizontal position with the head mouth downward.

The Sudarium, therefore, would have to have been placed on the disfigured head of a crucified man who was already dead. With the onset of *rigor mortis*, the pulmonary edema would begin to flow, soaking the beard and moustache. The body would then be taken down and placed on its right side, with pulmonary liquid continuing to flow from the nose, thus forming the stain that appears in the area of the forehead. By analyzing the formation of the "halos" that appear in the stains, each taking about 15 minutes to form, it can be determined that the victim was in a vertical position for approximately one hour, and in a horizontal position for about one more hour. This blood has been determined to be *post-mortem* blood, which means simply that it flowed after death had occurred. Acute pulmonary edema is characteristic of a person who has died of asphyxia after having been breathing with great difficulty as a consequence of his position during death.

If one of these principal stains is examined closely, for example that on the surface called *left reverse,* which actually came into contact with the face, it is possible to determine facial characteristics and the source of the flow of blood. It must be kept in mind that, being a mirror image, the left side of the stain corresponds with the right side of the face. It is also extremely important to remember that the stains were formed on a three-dimensional face, while the stain that appears on the cloth is extended on a plane. In order to see exactly how it conforms to a human face, it is necessary to wrinkle it once again to adjust it to the facial features. When that is done, one is able to see how the stained areas coincide with the central and right part of the forehead, the nose, the left cheek, and the area of the beard. The length of the nose has thus been measured at eight centimeters, with a projection of two centimeters at the base. All of the measurements taken (length and width of the nose, projection of the nose, and length of the face) correspond with those of a human face that is characteristic of the population of the Mediterranean area.

The group of stains that appears in the shape of dots is found in the area of the cloth that covered the base of the neck. It has been determined that they were formed by *vital* blood, which means that the blood flowed from these puncture wounds before death occurred, approximately one hour before the blood stained the cloth. They are consistent with the wounds that a crown of thorns could have produced.

A trapezoidal stain appears only on the first and second surfaces of the linen, and had to have been the last, or one of the last, to have formed. It is believed that it was formed by a closed fist, that was exerting pressure on the nose of the deceased in order to contain the flow of blood.

The stain in the form of butterfly wings corresponds to the area of the head where the hair was pulled back in the form of a "pigtail," stained with diluted blood.

There is also a "diffuse" stain, found between the principal stains and with a triangular shape. It is found only on the first and second surfaces of the linen. It is believed that this stain was caused by hair, stained and coagulated with blood, on which a diluted bloody solution was flowing slowly. It has been suggested that it was possibly produced by a superficial washing of the face, with the head resting on the cloth, or by diluted blood in the copious and agonizing sweat from asphyxia. This stain requires further study to determine the exact cause of formation.

Finger-shaped stains exist in distinct positions around the mouth and nose. Six different positions of various fingers of a left hand have been identified, produced when the linen had already been placed on the head. It is thought that they were produced when another person attempted to contain the flow of blood from the nose, both during the time when the body was being taken down from its vertical position, and while it was being transported to another location. These appear in successive waves, without any clear separation between them.

There is an "accordion" shaped stain, not as well defined as the others, that appears only on the third and fourth surfaces of the Sudarium. This stain was formed by saturation, later than the principal stains. Its upper border can be distinguished clearly, but the interior is much more diffused. Through experimentation, EDICES has obtained a stain with these characteristics by folding a cloth in the manner of a tube, and then applying it to another cloth with stains that were still damp. Greater definition was obtained in those areas where more pressure was exerted.

In addition to the stains in the shape of dots that appear in the area of the neck of the deceased, there are a great number of minuscule accessory stains that appear on almost the entire surface of the part of the cloth that directly came into contact with the body (the *left reverse*). Many of those that appear in the lower area, in the vicinity of the dot-shaped stains, are also of *vital* blood, which confirms once again that the Man of the Sudarium was already bloody before he died.

Conclusions of EDICES

According to Jorge-Manuel Rodríguez, EDICES can confirm at the present time the following conclusions:

1) The Sudarium of Oviedo has a series of stains originating from human blood, type AB.

2) The linen is wrinkled and dirty, partially torn, and burned. It is

stained and has a high degree of contamination, but does not show signs of fraudulent tampering or decay.

3) It is completely certain that it was placed on the head of the corpse of a normal adult male, who had a beard, moustache, and long hair, which was tied at the back of the head.

4) The subject was already dead, because the way in which the stains were formed is incompatible with any possible respiratory movement. Because of the composition of the stains, which have a proportion between blood and serum of one to six, it is certain that the man suffered a great pulmonary edema as a consequence of the dying process.

5) His mouth was almost closed, and the nose was pressed to the right from the pressure of the mortuary linen. The mouth and nose have been perfectly identified on the linen, and were the place of origin of the principal blood stains.

6) On the lower part of the left edge of the cloth are a series of stains which correspond to puncture wounds, produced while the man was still alive, which bled approximately one hour before the linen was placed on them.

7) Practically the entire head, neck, shoulders, and at least part of the back of this man were bloody prior to being covered by this linen, because the stains observed in the hair, forehead, and on the upper part of the head are of vital blood. It is certain that this man was mistreated before his death, with instruments that made him bleed from the scalp and which produced wounds on the neck, the shoulders and the upper part of the back.

CHAPTER SIX

HOW THE SUDARIUM WAS USED

EDICES made a replica of the Sudarium (a cloth with the shape of the stains drawn on it) and placed it on a model of a human head in order to prove how the areas of the Sudarium that are stained with blood correspond anatomically to a human head. As previously mentioned, the wrapping of the head was done twice, when the body was in two different positions. This was explained to me by Jorge-Manuel Rodríguez, and a translation of his article about this process, which appears in *LINTEUM*, the publication of EDICES, is summarized below.

The first position: The linen is placed on the head, partially wrapping it.

The linen of Oviedo was placed on the bloody head of a subject hanging in a vertical position, fastened with sharp objects (as can be seen by the small holes that can be observed on the cloth), beginning with the left part of the cloth. The cloth was then wrapped around the left part of the head up to the angle of the right jaw when, for reasons apparently unknown, the cloth was doubled back on itself (being folded double in the area of the face), and finished being wrapped with a few folds in the form of bellows at the angle of the left jaw. It is strange that the linen didn't totally wrap the head, most likely due to the fact that some obstacle impeded that operation. The obstacle in question well could have been the right arm of the cadaver, on which the right cheek was resting.

The lower part of the principal stain was formed with the body hanging in a vertical position. For this stain to be produced with the quantity of liquid and in the position that has been proven, it is necessary that the cadaver would have hung in a vertical position for approximately one hour, and that it had the right arm raised and the head inclined 70 degrees forward and 20 degrees to the right in relation to the vertical.

This position of the head *demands* a certain position of the entire body, which must be:

1) Suspended, with both arms in the form of a cross, because,

   • If he were hanging only from the right arm, the rest of the body, above all the head, would be in a position quite removed from this arm and inclined toward the left side, in a way incompatible with that of the head of the "man of the Sudarium."

   • These arms must be separated, because if he were hanging with the arms together on top of the head, the head would be inclined forward and not toward the right.

2) With both feet fastened, because if the body were simply hanging from the arms he would have died in 15 or 20 minutes, an insufficient amount of time to generate the quantity of liquid necessary to form the stains that are found on the linen.

Therefore, the position compatible with the way in which the stains of the Oviedo cloth were formed is that in which both arms are fastened and separated above the head, and with the feet in a position which makes it very difficult to breathe. It is a position completely analogous to that of a crucified man. It can be said that the "man of the Sudarium of Oviedo" was first mistreated and later "crucified."

The upper part of the principal stain was formed with the body in a horizontal position. Later, without altering the position of the arms, the cadaver was placed in a lateral right prone position, maintaining the turn of the head 20 degrees to the right and placing it at 115 degrees with respect to the vertical, with the forehead supported on a hard surface, a position which was maintained for about one hour more. This makes one suppose that the body was taken from its vertical position, and placed in a horizontal position that is almost face down.

The minor stains appear on top of the principal stains during the transport of the body: After the time mentioned had passed, the cadaver was moved while the left hand of another person, in various positions from above the body, tried to contain the flow of hematic serum through the nose and mouth, with firm pressure on these parts of the body. It is at this time when the small minor stains, superimposed on the lower part of the principal stain, were formed. This process lasted five minutes.

Second position: The linen wraps the head completely.

Until this moment the linen remained doubled over the face of the cadaver. But, in a determined moment (as soon as the obstacle that impeded it disappeared), the linen was unfolded and enveloped the entire head of the cadaver, which was perfectly covered by this sort of *capucha* or hood that remained fastened to the hair with sharp objects.

This hood formed a sort of cone, knotted at the top of the head, and whose base reached to the upper part of the back of this person. With the head thus covered, one last movement was made of the body, with the face positioned downward and supported on the left fist of a hand that was positioned so that the front of the hand was facing upward. This movement produced the great stain in the form of a triangle, on whose surface are clearly visible the fingers of the hand that was in contact with the cloth, as well as the curve inscribed on the cheek by the part that was in contact with the face. In a way similar to that previously described, this movement had to have taken place in about five or ten minutes maximum.

A little slippage of the linen on the face in this position is also noticeable, because some of the stains appear to be duplicated.

Finally, for unknown reasons, the body was placed on its back, and immediately the linen was removed from the head and covered with aloe and myrrh. The micro-photographs show particles of these elements stuck to the bloody areas, which indicates that the linen was covered with these elements after having been stained with blood, and before the stains dried.

The results are perfectly compatible with the hypothesis that the cadaver was that of Jesus of Nazareth, and have led to an extensive comparative study between the Shroud of Turin and the Sudarium by the investigative team of CES.

CHAPTER SEVEN

CARBON 14 AND
THE SUDARIUM

I n an article published in LINTEUM, as well as in his book *The Oviedo Cloth*, Mark Guscin investigates the question of carbon dating. As previously mentioned, EDICES is not certain if, when, or under what conditions a carbon 14 dating was carried out on the Sudarium of Oviedo, and does not consider it to be a relevant factor in determining the authenticity of the cloth. According to Guscin's investigation, the first reference to carbon dating and the Sudarium was made at an international seminar on the Shroud, held in Barcelona in 1991. Because of a contribution made by the speaker, Mario Moroni, it was made public that the dating of the Sudarium of Oviedo had attributed to the cloth a date that fit between the first and the seventh century, a date that is not at all exact. Later, in 1994, it was reported at the First International Congress on the Sudarium in Oviedo that Mario Moroni sent two laboratories, that of the University of Arizona in Tucson and the ISO Trace Radiocarbon Laboratory of Toronto, fragments of the Sudarium taken by Max Frei in 1979. According to this report, the results of the dating were between 642 and 869 (Tucson) and 653-786 (Toronto) with 95% reliability. A short time later many reports were published which said that Dr. Baime Bollone had a highly contaminated sample dated in Tucson and that the result showed that the cloth dated from the second half of the first millennium, between 500 and 1000 AD. When Guscin wrote to Tucson to clarify matters, they wrote back saying that they had received two samples of the Sudarium as CO_2 gas in ampoules that had leaked air and were therefore unusable. According to the lab, the carbon dating was not carried out.

Wondering why Dr. Bollone would report very specific results that do not support what he believes, Guscin continued his investigation. In 1997, at a Shroud convention in San Marino, Mario Moroni said that the samples were sent to the Tucson laboratory about one year apart; both ampoules had an identification number, but the original and supposed historical dates were kept secret. He also produced a letter from the laboratory of the University of Arizona that contains the results that were published in the Acts of the Congress of Oviedo. Another letter from the same laboratory, dated two years later and signed by another person, says that the sample tested was that of a linen cloth, Copta tomb, and gives dates between 540 and 754 AD with 95% reliability. The identification number disagrees with those of the first letter, and the description of the cloth is completely erroneous. When questioned about it, Dr. Jull wrote back from the Tucson laboratory that the two results did not appear to him to be in disagreement, that they had material remaining from the samples, and that "in order to produce a radiocarbon date on any particular material, it is important that the origin of the samples be known and clearly stated to the laboratory." He claimed that they had been informed that the second sample, the one supposedly from a Coptic tomb, was from the eleventh century. He that said that he didn't think that the correct protocol was followed and suggested doing a "serious" dating.

It should also be mentioned that the samples were not taken with permission for radiocarbon dating, and had been taken from the cloth about 15 years before being sent to Tucson. It is not known in what condition they were kept during that time.

What is obvious is that the radiocarbon results published in the Acts of the First International Congress on the Sudarium of Oviedo are without scientific value, and cannot be considered as a factor when discussing the authenticity of the cloth.

As stated at the beginning, the investigative team of CES began their studies on the Sudarium of Oviedo in 1989, after it was announced that carbon 14 dating of the Shroud of Turin had definitively dated it from 1260 to 1390. Their objective was to find out if the Sudarium of Oviedo and the Shroud of Turin had indeed covered the same person, because if this were the case, the carbon dating results would have to be erroneous. It is absolutely certain that the Sudarium was in Oviedo in 1075, and that it had been in Spain for several centuries prior to that date. All of the studies carried out to date on the Sudarium indicate that it covered the same crucifixion victim as the Shroud of Turin. While the objective of this book is not to discuss the Shroud in a detailed manner, subsequent scientific studies on this burial cloth have uncovered many possible reasons for error, which include the following.

First of all, while carbon dating has a reputation with the public of being a very simple and accurate method, it is not. It has never been considered to be infallible by reputable scientists, and has a long history of mistaken dates and embarrassing errors. Mark Guscin gives several examples in his book, *The Oviedo Cloth*. According to him, in one of the three laboratories responsible for the dating of the Shroud, located in Zurich, the head of the laboratory dated a sample taken from a 50-year-old tablecloth in his mother-in-law's house. The results said that it was three hundred and fifty years old. In another case, the Oxford laboratory gave an estimated age of 1,200 years for some South African rock paintings, discovered by a school boy. When the results were published, a 72-year-old woman recognized the painting as her own work of art, done only eleven years before. It had been stolen and discarded in the bush. Another laboratory involved in the dating of the Shroud, that of Tucson, Arizona, dated a Viking horn to the year 2006 AD. Carbon dating has also dated the bones of a mummy in Manchester approximately a thousand years older than the bandages. The examples mentioned by Guscin are innumerable, and all point to the fact that carbon dating is an imperfect science, especially in the presence of any contamination on the sample. Both the Sudarium of Oviedo and the Shroud of Turin have a high degree of contamination due to the fact that they are ancient cloths, traditionally exposed for veneration without any protection whatsoever.

Contrary to the way carbon dating has been portrayed by the media, as a foolproof scientific method, archaeologists do not share this attitude toward its accuracy. For example, the Biblical archaeologist Dr. Eugenia Nitowski has expressed nearly the same sentiments as EDICES, quoted at the beginning of this chapter. This is logic, and would reflect the opinion of any reputable scientist or educated person:

In any form of inquiry or scientific discipline, it is the weight of evidence which must be considered conclusive. In archaeology, if there are ten lines of evidence, carbon-dating being one of them, and it conflicts with the other nine, there is little hesitation to throw out the carbon date as inaccurate due to unforeseen contamination[1].

The highly respected Greek archaeologist Spyros Iakovidis shares this view, and feels "that this method is not exactly to be trusted." On one occasion he sent a certain amount of the same burnt grain to two different laboratories in two different parts of the world. The readings differed by two thousand years, with the correct archaeological date being in the middle[2].

Many scientists have also developed theories that may be able to explain the erroneous dating of the Shroud of Turin. For example, two Russian doctors from the Moscow Laboratory of Physico-Chemical Research believe that linen has special characteristics that can affect its radiocarbon content, and that would make them seem to be younger than they really are. During manufacture of the linen, the waxes and fats from the original flax are lost, giving the remaining fibers a higher level of carbon 14 atoms. This explains why the bandages of the mummy in Manchester would be dated a thousand years younger than the bones.

Other scientists, including Dr. John Jackson of Colorado Springs, believe that the high temperature during the fire of 1532 would have enriched the carbon 14 content of the Shroud. Another theory is that of Dr. Leoncio A. Garza-Valdés[3], who discovered that an organic "bioplastic coating" is created over time on ancient textiles, including the Shroud. This coating distorts the carbon dating process, making linens appear to be much younger than they actually are, and would also explain the difficulties encountered in the dating of Egyptian burial cloths. In experiments he demonstrated that only about 10% of this coating is affected by the cleaning methods used by the laboratories involved in the dating of the Shroud of Turin.

While these hypotheses are currently being tested, the conclusion that can be reached is that carbon dating is not, and has never been, an exact science. It was rarely mentioned in the media until the public announcement in the late 1980s was made that carbon dating had "proved" that the Shroud of Turin was a medieval fake, acquiring overnight status as the one infallible method that had finally disproved

---

[1] Ian Wilson, *British Society for the Turin Shroud*, Newsletter No. 30 (Dec. 1991/Jan. 1992): 5-8.

[2] *Ibid*, (Dec. 1991/Jan. 1992): 8.

[3] *The DNA of God?* (New York: Doubleday, 1999).

the literally hundreds of other scientific conclusions that had been reached during the many years of Shroud studies. This sort of reporting is irresponsible and completely contrary to logic and scientific reasoning. The only possible explanation is that the Shroud of Turin has an image of Jesus those origin cannot be explained by modern science. It not only authenticates the passion and death of the historical Jesus, but also appears to be living proof of His resurrection, and this is unacceptable for the hedonistic and materialistic mentality of modern-day Western culture. For many it appears to be preferable to deny the supernatural power of Jesus, and even the historical facts of His life, because this seems to absolve them from the responsibility contained in Christian doctrine.

On October 13, 1988, Cardinal Anastasio Ballestero, who was at that time Archbishop of Turin and Pontifical Custodian of the Shroud, held a press conference at which he read a statement concerning the dating of the cloth by the three laboratories. In response to a journalist's question: "Why have you trusted science?" Cardinal Ballestero replied:

Because science has asked for our trust. We all know very well the accusation science levels against the Church has always been that the Church fears science because science's 'truth' is superior to the Church's. Hence, to let science have its say seems to me to have been the Christian thing to do... Science has spoken; now science will have to evaluate its results... The Church is calm, has been and remains firm in insisting that the cult of the Holy Shroud will go on and that veneration for this sacred linen will remain one of the treasures of our Church... The Shroud has entered the liturgy of a Church; that shows how important and how efficacious it is. Science must speak as it finds; it is all too clear that what it has said is far from being the last word about this enigmatic sheet which evokes the face of Christ, and not the face alone, but the mystery of the Lord's passion and death, and probably his resurrection too.[4]

---

[4] From *La Voce del Popolo*, November 6, 1988. Also appears in *The Shroud: A Guide*, by Gino Moretto (New York: Paulist Press, 1998).

Cardinal Ballestero was right. Science, in the years since 1988, has evaluated its results by studying the carbon dating process, especially as it relates to linens and specifically to the Shroud of Turin, finding in the process many reasons for error. In the meantime, the Shroud is more enigmatic and popular than ever, with the subsequent publication of many more books that insist on its authenticity, based on the innumerable other scientific tests that have been performed to date. Many scientists, such as Dr. John Jackson of Colorado Springs and Gilbert R. Lavoie, M.D., have dedicated more than 20 years of their lives to its study, and are more convinced than ever that the cloth is not only authentic, but that it may contain the imprint of the Resurrection of Jesus.

CHAPTER EIGHT

THE SHROUD
AND THE SUDARIUM:
COMPARATIVE STUDIES

The comparative study of the Shroud of Turin and the Sudarium of Oviedo shows that the frontal stains on the sudarium have seventy points of coincidence with the Shroud, according to the image overlay technique used by Dr. Alan Whanger. He has concluded that both cloths covered the face of the same person. It should be remembered that the first person to notice the similarities of both cloths was Monsignor Ricci. The comparative study of the two cloths can be summarized as follows.

The weave. The linen of Oviedo has a taffeta weave, while the Shroud is a linen weave of serge or herringbone. This means that the linen of Oviedo is coarser and was probably used for domestic purposes, as a cloth to wipe the sweat from the face, to wear on the head as a turban, or possibly as a scarf or towel. The Shroud, on the other hand, is a more expensive cloth that probably came from Syria, specifically from the oasis around the city of Palmyra, and was the type of weave used for the shrouding of the diseased.

Blood type. The blood of both cloths is type AB, a blood group common in the Middle East and rare in Europe.

Facial characteristics. a) The nose on both the Shroud and the Sudarium has been measured at eight centimeters, or a little more than three inches. The nasal area on both cloths contains a high degree of dirt and dust. The nose is swollen in the middle of the right side and is somewhat displaced to the right. This was typical of crucifixion victims, because the horizontal bar of the cross was placed across the back of the neck and was possibly even tied to the arms. When the person fell, which was frequent due to his weakened condition after the scourging, he was not able to protect his face from the impact of the fall. b) The right cheek is not represented on either cloth due to the contusion that can be seen in this area, while the area of the right cheek is completely bloody on both cloths. c) Correspondence can be seen between the point of the nose and nasal cavities, the position and size of the mouth, the chin, and the shape of the beard.

Bloodstains. The bloodstains have geometrically compatible sizes and have very similar positions on both linens. The stains are of human blood of the group AB. A DNA study is pending analysis on both cloths, due to the difficulties caused by ancient blood and scarce cellularity. The stains produced from *vital* blood, those produced by the puncture wounds at the back of the neck, are the same on both linens. Remember that the linen of Oviedo was fastened to the head in the back with sharply pointed objects, perhaps thorns. The cloth fell on the left shoulder and upper part of the back of the person, and wrapped the left part of the face. This entire area that was touched by the cloth was completely bloody before blood flowed from the nose and mouth after death had occurred. There is a notable similarity between both linens in the back part of the head, which match essentially in size, position, and genesis, which means that both contain *vital* blood, or blood which flowed before the death of the victim. In addition, the blood stains on the back of both linens correspond, found on the two right and left lower corners on the Oviedo cloth.

Other similarities. The Shroud wrapped the body of a man who was crucified after having been scourged and crowned with thorns. The Sudarium of Oviedo also wrapped the body of a person whose death is perfectly compatible with crucifixion, scourging, and crowning with thorns. Both deaths, then, are completely analogous, and while the scourging was normal procedure for crucifixion victims, the crowning with thorns was not. The only mention of a crowning with thorns is that found in the Biblical accounts of the passion of Jesus of Nazareth.

The Shroud completely wrapped the body of a man, including the head. The Sudarium of Oviedo completely wrapped the head of a man, lightly resting on the shoulders, especially the left one, and on the back. There is a nearly identical match between the stains of blood on the Shroud with those on the Sudarium, keeping in mind that there is a lateral displacement on the Shroud, which has been described by Dr. John Jackson. This will be discussed further in the fourth part of the book, which discusses chapter 20 of the Gospel of John, but here it is sufficient to say that this displacement becomes greater the farther the stains are from the middle plane of the face, and cannot be explained in terms of current scientific knowledge.

Conclusions

Based on the marked similarity between the Shroud of Turin and the Sudarium of Oviedo, it can be said the probability that they did not cover the same person is extremely small. According to EDICES, what probability exists that both formations of stains, generated by chance and at different times with different subjects, would be able to demonstrate this much similarity? If one adds to the physical and geometrical similarities those such as the similarities in how long it took the stains to form, as well as historical considerations, one would be left with only one explanation: that both linens were placed on the same person, and that that person was Jesus of Nazareth, a Jew crucified at noon in Jerusalem during the rule of the Roman governor Pontius Pilate, and who died three hours later. As will be seen in the next chapter about Jewish burial ritual, cultural considerations also point to the same conclusion. The possibility that the relic was falsified would be remote, illogical, against the ideas of the epoch, and quite impossible due to the lack of knowledge about physio-pathological processes.

For the benefit of those who still believe in the possibility that some unscrupulous people could indeed have either found the grave cloths of another victim of crucifixion or deliberately crucified someone in order to obtain fraudulent relics, I would like to point out just how impossible this would be.

First of all, crucifixion was a Roman method of punishment, and their victims were left on the cross for days, often until the body began to rot. The legs were normally broken (Jn 19:32), and the bodies were then thrown into mass graves, without a proper burial and certainly without the use of a shroud, sudarium, and other burial cloths. Jesus was an exception, and if not the *only* crucified man to be granted a proper Jewish burial in a tomb, He was certainly one of few. He was also the only victim mentioned who was crowned with thorns, which was really a cap of thorns placed on His head in order to mock the claim that He was the Messiah. Crucifixion was banned in the year 313 by the Emperor Constantine, long before the medieval falsification of relics.

The demand for relics was a phenomenon of the Middle Ages, due to the expectation of miracles associated with these objects, as well as an increased devotion to the saints. The Sudarium, however, was already in Oviedo and had been for several centuries. Most of the falsification was being done with types of relics that lent themselves easily to this sort of thing: thorns, nails, hair, bones, tears, the Virgin's milk, bread from the Last Supper and Jesus' miracle, bits of fabric, wood from the manger, stones from the tomb, Calvary, or other important places, earth that Jesus had stepped upon, manna from the desert, and even such unlikely things as the mud God used to create Adam, or the feathers of angels. There are also copies of the Turin Shroud, and innumerable veils of Veronica; these are quite easy to distinguish as being artistic representations, however, and none has merited serious study. Nevertheless, along with the questionable relics exist those that are indeed authentic. It is unlikely that anyone would have taken great pains to falsify a relic when it was so easy to paint an image on cloth, or present bread, stones, feathers and mud as being authentic and religiously significant for the unsophisticated and rather gullible populace of the medieval world. If anyone had dared to falsify a blood relic of Jesus, it would have just as effective to saturate a cloth with the blood of an animal, because the world was not capable of distinguishing the difference. Why would anyone actually crucify someone when scientific methodology at that time was practically non-existent? It was certainly not known that some day in the future scientists would be capable of DNA, pollen, and other testing that could determine authenticity. It is absurd to think that the Templars or other Christians would have resorted to murder, especially when it was not necessary.

Once again, it is quite certain that the authentic Sudarium and Shroud of Jesus would have been safeguarded by the apostles and other disciples. If, in the highly unlikely scenario that they had lost them, it would have been impossible to find similar cloths, and, furthermore, would have been completely contrary to their mentality. It is impossible to imagine the disciples of Jesus spending their time rummaging through tombs in the futile hope of finding the bloodstained burial cloths of another crucifixion victim who had been exempted from the Roman regulations. They would have been arrested and Christianity would never have survived. Nor would these cloths have had any significance for Christians. It appears that the Shroud and the Sudarium were not exposed for veneration by the faithful for many hundreds of years, and only on rare occasions, so there would be no reason to fabricate these relics in order to attract pilgrims.

The Sudarium and the Shroud were saved and venerated only because they contained the sacred blood and the sacred image of Christ. It is not logical to assume that the early Christians would have preserved the blood-soaked burial cloths of a common criminal, saving them from the Persians and later from the Arabs. It defies explanation how they would have been able to find a shroud with an image of the historical Jesus when scientists today are unable to duplicate it.

Mark Guscin also points out that the idea that Christians would have deliberately crucified someone in direct imitation of Jesus would have been sacrilegious to the medieval mind, not to mention the blasphemy of then placing the "relics" thus obtained in cathedrals for public veneration. The naked image that appears on the Shroud of Turin was in violation of the ethics of the time, and the bloody forms found on the Sudarium of Oviedo were hardly suitable for veneration.

Furthermore, as Guscin points out, the idea that someone could have found unused ancient burial cloths, taken them through all of the countries in which the real relics had been in order to obtain the proper mix of pollens, crucified a victim with Semitic features who happened to cooperate by dying in exactly the same manner and time frame as Christ, and then successfully obtained an image either during the burial process or from an artist that would continue to defy scientific explanation in the 21st century is ludicrous. This "crucifixion" also would have had to be carried out in utmost secrecy, in order to avoid historical mention of such a fraudulent and horrific endeavor. While some may continue to believe that people were capable of this sort of fraud, it was not only unnecessary, but also impossible according to science, nature, and history.

There is one more consideration. That is that the Shroud of Turin was supposedly "dated" to the thirteenth century, while the Sudarium of Oviedo has been in Spain since the seventh century. This means, of course, that the so-called fraud would have had to have occurred twice, and that the wounds, facial characteristics, manner of death, pollen, and other evidence on both relics would have to match exactly. This, quite frankly, would be impossible, since the Sudarium of Oviedo was not removed from its chest in the thirteenth century, not even for kings, not to mention the fact that its use was unknown at that time. Blood typing, forensic medicine, pollen identification, the electronic scan microscope, photography, and all of the other scientific means at our disposal today did not exist. Microscopic information cannot be falsified, and it is for that reason that criminals are convicted today on the basis of DNA, fibers, and other evidence, because it is indisputable.

It appears to be evident that the Shroud of Turin and the Sudarium of Oviedo, although separated for most of their history, had been placed on the same human victim of crucifixion. The bloodstains, blood type, manner of death, facial characteristics and other considerations not only match on both cloths, but are also consistent with the Biblical accounts of the passion, death, and burial of Jesus. Their study has engaged the efforts of more than forty dedicated and reputable scientists for many, many years, who have not been able to find a single piece of evidence that would prove the invalidity of the cloths, not even the radiocarbon testing, due to the many problems already mentioned. In fact, the image on the Shroud of Turin continues to be an enigma in an age that claims to be able to accomplish almost anything, from travel in outer space to the cloning of animals. Nevertheless, in an otherwise intelligent and sophisticated society, the idea of medieval falsification keeps resurfacing, based not on science, logic, and reason, but rather on the inability to believe.

PART THREE

THE SUDARIUM AND JEWISH FUNERARY RITES

Since the life of a living body is in its blood,

I have made you put it on the altar,

So that atonement may thereby be made for your own lives,

Because it is the blood, as the seat of life,

that makes atonement.

LEVITICUS 17:11

CHAPTER NINE

JEWISH BELIEFS ABOUT DEATH, BLOOD AND MOURNING

Does what we now know about the Sudarium of Oviedo coincide with Jewish burial rites of the first century? The answer is that there appears to be nothing known about first century rituals that would eliminate the possibility that this is the authentic face cloth of Jesus of Nazareth. On the contrary, Jewish ritual with regard to death and burial not only supports the authenticity of the cloth, but also sheds much light on many aspects of the burial that have been troubling, such as whether or not the body was washed, at what point the sudarium was used and later removed from the head, and if the preparation was complete or precipitated. This chapter will discuss ancient Jewish funerary rites and how they apply to the death of Jesus, comparing these also with what is now known about the Sudarium of Oviedo and the Shroud of Turin.

The first thing to be discussed is the Jewish idea of death, which influenced their behavior with the dead, as well as their great respect for death. Man appears as a creature of God in ancient religions, but in Judaism he is made in the image and likeness of God (Gn 1:26-27). Nevertheless, he is a mortal and sinful creature, who cannot escape the finality of death. Man is clay who lives by the breath of God (Gn 2:7); when God recalls the breath of life, man must yield his spirit. The soul and the flesh are two principles that are fused together in a human being. Consciousness is diffused throughout the body, and when death occurs, there is no separation of the two[1]. It was commonly believed that the dead continued to exist in Sheol, in a languid, non-dynamic existence, which was destined to end in a relatively brief period of time, but only if certain conditions were fulfilled: a) A normal life span must be attained, 70 years according to Psalms 90:10, b) The deceased must leave children to perpetuate his name, and c) the person must be buried in a sepulcher, in order to avoid the possibility that he might disturb the balance between the world of the living and that of the dead. If one of these conditions was not fulfilled, death became a problem for the Jews. A premature death was thought to be a punishment inflicted by powers other than Yahweh. These destructive powers rule the domain of death, Sheol, where it is not possible to praise God (Is 38:18), and where the recollection of God has been annihilated (Ps 6:5). Because death could not exist as a destructive force next to a living, omnipotent God, life had to absorb death (cf. II Co 5:4)[2].

After being deprived of life, separated from the world of the living, and exiled to Sheol, the domain of the destructive powers, the dead person becomes *impure*. Contact with him must be avoided, and everything related to him as well. For this reason, as well as the Jewish belief that death was not total destruction, it was considered to be the worst of curses to remain unburied and at the mercy of the birds and beasts of the fields (Ps 79:2; Jr. 16:4; Ezk 29:5; 1K 14:11). Isaiah 14:18-20 is the satire of the death of the king of Babylon, which expresses the horror of a death without burial:

> All the kings of the nations lie in glory, each in his own tomb; But you are cast forth without burial, loathsome and corrupt, clothed as those slain at sword-point, a trampled corpse. Going down to the pavement of the pit, you will never be one with them in the grave.

For reasons of legal purity, the law ordered burying the executed:

> If a man guilty of a capital offense is put to death and his corpse hung on a tree, it shall not remain on the tree overnight. You shall bury it the same day; otherwise, since God's curse rests on him who hangs on a tree, you

---

[1] See John L. McKenzie, *Dictionary of the Bible* (New York: MacMillan, 1965): 538-539.

[2] *The Interpreter's Dictionary of the Bible* (Nashville: Abingdon Press, 1962), Vol. 1.

will defile the land which the Lord, your God, is giving you as an inheritance" (Dt 21:22-23).

It was only by burying the dead that impurity would disappear from the earth (Ezk 39:12-16). According to this Jewish law, it was absolutely necessary that Jesus be buried before sunset. The Romans, on the other hand, normally left their victims on the cross for days, often until the body began to decompose or was eaten by birds and other animals. This was, of course, repulsive and unthinkable for the Jewish mentality, and as it says in Deuteronomy, was not permitted even in the case of crucifixion.

Although it was believed that a person became impure through contact with the deceased, the living were required to carefully prepare the corpse for a proper burial in a sepulcher. This was important because death was *not* considered to be total destruction; the dead person was destined for a provisional state of being in Sheol, and sin was expiated through the deterioration of the flesh. Therefore, the Jews were quite preoccupied with the rituals of the funeral ceremony, with the intention of granting every human being a burial worthy of one made in the image and likeness of God. This was true even in the case of criminals, although, as will be explained later, criminals executed by order of the Jewish court were interred in a special cemetery and were not mourned.

Despite censure, the dead were not lost to the living. Their presence within the family was thought to continue, and gifts were frequently deposited upon or next to the grave, an action that presupposed a certain belief in existence in the afterlife. The dead were thought to be able to eat and communicate with their visitors, and could even appear to the living, as for example in the Biblical account of Samuel's appearance to Saul, who asks, "Why do you disturb me by conjuring me up?" (1 Sam 28:15) Nevertheless, Saul himself prohibited necromancy and divination; departed souls could appear to the living only with the permission of God.

The Importance of Blood

According to the study done by Florentino Díez[3], Genesis mentions several gestures that were practiced immediately after death, common in all of the countries of the ancient Near East until after the first century. Some have even continued until the present day: the eyes were closed (46:4), the arms were laid out on the body, and the body was kissed (50:1). The Mishnah, the oldest post-biblical collection of Jewish oral laws[4], states that other precautions were to be taken in order to delay the decomposition of the body, due to the heat of the region of Palestine: the nose and ears were closed, and the jaw was tied with a strip of cloth so that it would not drop. The body was then "anointed and washed" according to Mishnaic regulations, although the order varies according to the source. Díez believes that it is most probable that there was a first anointing before washing the body with water, followed by a second anointing with perfumed essences. The body was finally wrapped in a clean linen sheet or *sindon*, and additional spices were placed inside.

As Rebecca Jackson, Associate Director of the Turin Shroud Center of Colorado[5], points out, the bloodstains that appear on the Shroud of Turin indicate that the body of the Man of the Shroud was not washed. She states that this fact is in "total compliance" with Halachah or Jewish law, according to which a Jewish man or woman may not undergo ritual purification if one or more of the following conditions exist:

a) *The person was a victim of a violent death and/or blood flowed during his or her lifetime and continued to flow at the time of death,* b) *The deceased received capital punishment for a crime of a religious nature,* c) *The candidate for burial was an outcast from the Jewish community, and* d) *If the deceased was assassinated by a non-Jew.*

If this Man of the Shroud were Jesus, of course, he would have been

---

[3] Doctor in Biblical Science, Ex-Director of the Spanish Biblical Institute and Archaeologist of Jerusalem. His article appears in *Actas del I Congreso sobre el Sudario de Oviedo.*

[4] The Mishna was compiled by scholars over a period of two centuries, and was finished early in the 3rd century AD by Judah Ha-Nasi.

[5] "Jewish Burial Procedures at the Time of Christ," published in *Actas del I Congreso sobre el Sudario de Oviedo,* 1996.

disqualified under all four conditions. According to this law, a woman who dies while giving birth, for example, must not be cleaned if she had lost much blood. Jesus would have been simply anointed and wrapped in a *sindon,* or shroud, which is supported by scientific studies on the Shroud of Turin that indicate that the body was not washed.

The reason for this exception is the Jewish concept of blood, the life of the living being (Gn 9:4, Dt 12:23), as well as their concept of death. Blood was the "seat of life or of the soul," and became the "object of sacred awe[6]." In the case of a large loss of blood, as with Jesus, it would have been imperative to preserve the blood with aloes and myrrh and refrain from washing it away. Blood was an essential element of the body, fused with the concept of the flesh (Lv 17). Blood, as the "seat of life" (Lv 17:11) was essential for atonement, and therefore necessary for existence in Sheol. As Jorge-Manuel Rodríguez has pointed out, the blood was thought to contain the soul of the person. The imprint of the hand placed on the Sudarium of Oviedo in order to contain the flow of blood would therefore be a perfectly logical procedure, done to prevent the soul from leaving the body.

Studies on the Sudarium indicate that the cloth was removed from the face of the deceased in order to carry out the first rites of anointing, was covered with these spices before the blood on it had dried, and was placed elsewhere in the tomb. As mentioned previously, the sudarium had been wrapped a second time while the body was in a horizontal position, this time completely surrounding the head in the form of a hood, knotted at the top. According to their studies, this knot was left in place, so that when the cloth was later seen by Peter and John, it would have had the appearance of being "rolled up." Interestingly enough, these observations serve to explain the frequently debated passage of John 20:5-7 concerning the position of the linens. The sudarium was indeed placed "apart" from the shroud on Friday afternoon. When the apostles saw it on Sunday morning, it was in "its place" or in "the same place" it had been before.

The Jewish concept of blood also explains why the apostles would

---

[6] *The Jewish Encyclopedia,* p. 259.

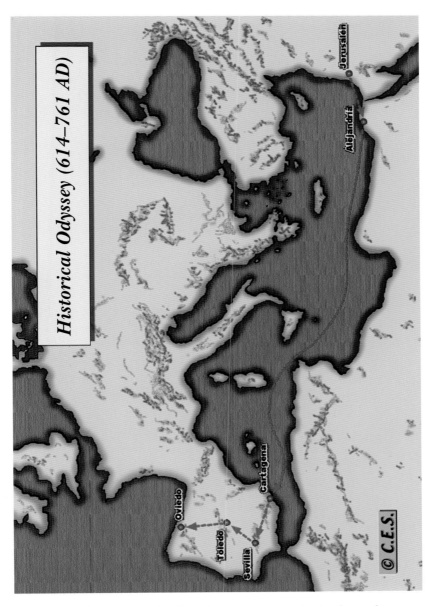

1. Historical odyssey of the *Arca Santa* from Jerusalem to Spain, due to the Persian invasion of 614 AD. The final destination of the chest is Oviedo, arriving in the year 761.

2. San Salvador, the Cathedral of Oviedo in Asturias, Spain.

© Jorge M. Rodríguez. (CES)

3. The *Cámara Santa*, or Holy Chamber, of the Cathedral of Oviedo, built in the 8th century by Alfonso II for the holy chest of relics.

4. Benediction with the Sudarium of Oviedo on September 14, 1999.

5.a. The lower hermitage on Monsacro, the sacred mountain where it is believed that the relics were kept for fifty years.

5.b. Our Lady of Monsagro, the upper hermitage of Monsacro that served as the hiding place for the relics during the Moorish invasion of Spain, from 711-761 AD.

6.a. Close up view of Our Lady of Monsagro.

6.b. Interior of the Hermitage of Our Lady of Monsagro. The relics were hidden in the "Well of St. Toribio," which can be seen on the right.

7.a. Monastery of St. Toribio of Liébana in Picos de Europa, which is believed to safeguard the largest fragment of the True Cross in the world.

7.b. The relic of the True Cross, exposed for veneration in its gold casing.

8. Altar in which the relic of the True Cross is safeguarded.

9. Engraving of the year 1722, the work of Gaspar Massi, which features St. Toribio, Bishop of Astorga, holding the True Cross, with the Monastery and its surroundings in the background.

10.a. An example of one of the many types of pollen found on the Sudarium.

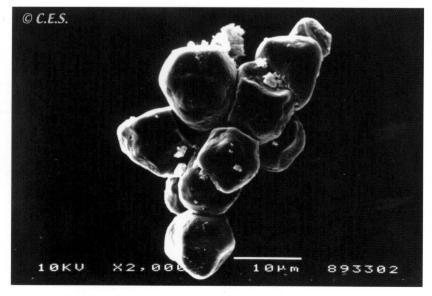

10b. Particles of aloe and myrrh, found attached to the blood, which indicates that they were applied to the cloth before the blood had dried completely.

11.a. Obverse side of the Sudarium, as it is currently being shown to the public.

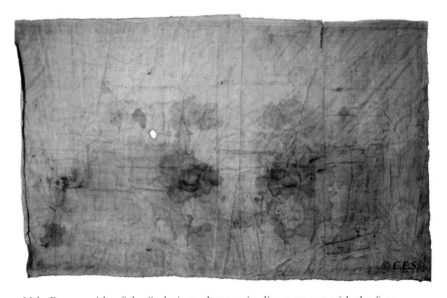

11.b. Reverse side of the Sudarium, that was in direct contact with the face.

12. Diagonal folds in the corner of the Sudarium, and on a model used for comparison.

13. Speculated inversion. The "Principal Stain 1" is that which was in contact with the face, and appears inverted as in a mirror.

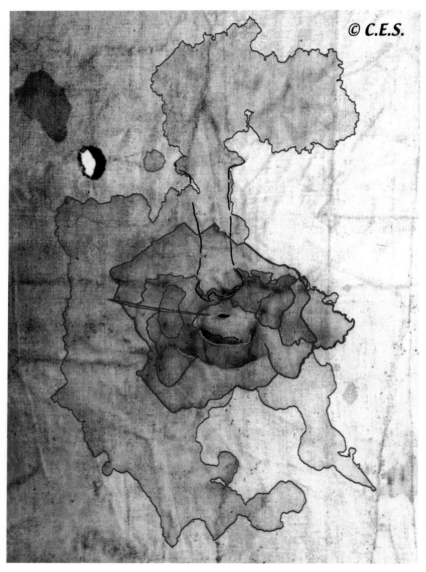

14. The principal stain of the left reverse side of the cloth, that was in contact
with the face. The outline of the trapezoidal stain is evident surrounding the area
that corresponds to the nose and mouth. Within this area the finger-shaped stains
are outlined on both sides of the mouth and the lower part of the nose. The
forehead stain can be seen to the upper right of the burn hole.

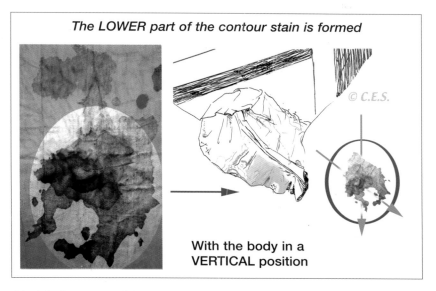

15.a. The lower part of the principal stain is formed with the body in a vertical position.

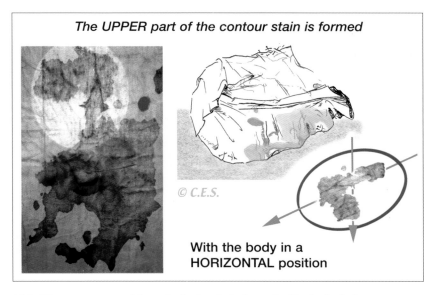

15.b. The upper part of the principal stain is formed with the body in a horizontal position.

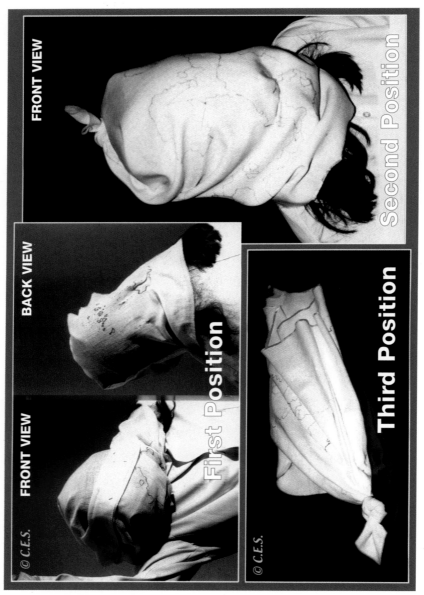

16. Positions of the linen. The Sudarium was placed over the head, first in a vertical position, and then when the body was placed horizontally on a flat surface. The final position shows how the cloth was left after being removed from the head.

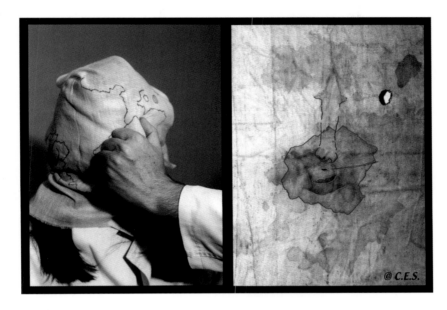

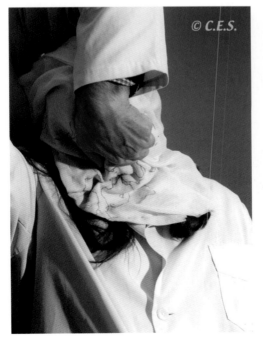

17.a. The trapezoidal stain was generated by a left hand that applied pressure to the nasal area in order to contain the flow of blood.

17.b. Finger-shaped stains were formed when the same left hand, inverting its position, embraces the nose between the thumb and index finger, also to contain the blood flow.

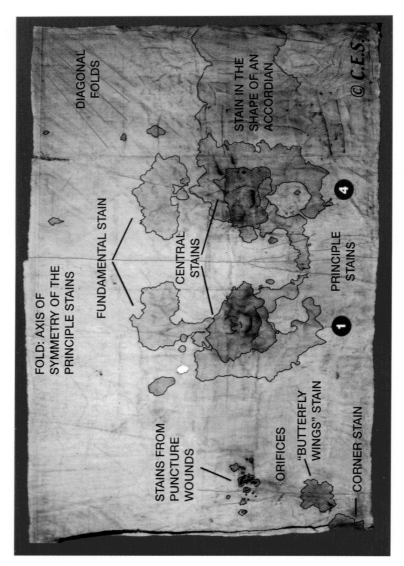

18. Denominations of the major stains on the reverse side of the Sudarium. The puncture wound stains, stain in the shape of butterfly wings, and the corner stain can be seen to the lower left of the cloth. The principal stains are visible on both sides of the central fold, with the accordion stain to the right. The diagonal wrinkles are in the upper right corner. The center fold forms the axis of symmetry for the principal stains.

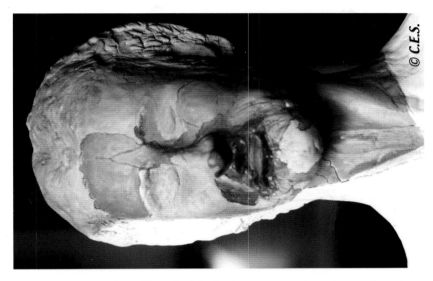

19.a. Bust 1. Front view of how the bloodstains correspond to a human head in three dimensions.

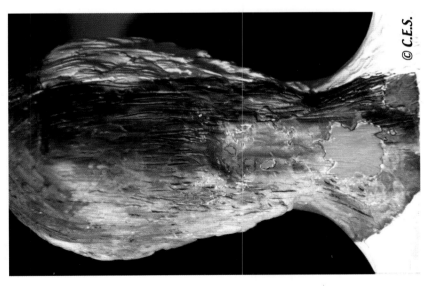

19.b. Bust 2. Back view.

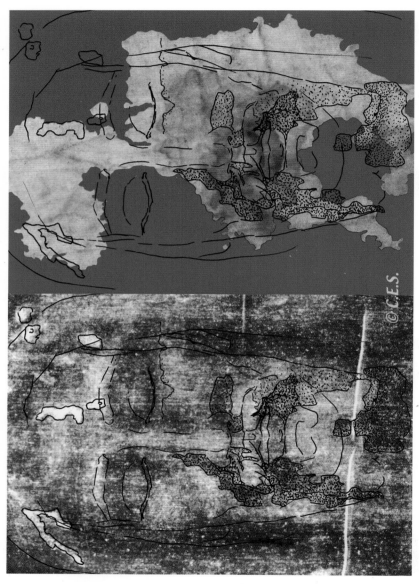

20. Comparison of the Sudarium of Oviedo and the Shroud of Turin. A clotted flow of blood appears on the right side of both linens, extending the length of the beard. It is post-mortem blood on both cloths, with a very similar morphology, measured at 1,310 mm² on the Shroud and 1,980 mm² on the Sudarium.

he appears to have done everything in his power to convince the chief priests and the elders to release Jesus, and even washes his hands of the matter. The Romans might have been concerned if Jesus had political aspirations, but, on the contrary, the Messiah always spoke as a kind and gentle philosopher, proclaiming that his kingdom was not of this world. The Jews, on the other hand, insist that according to their law he must die, because he made himself the Son of God, to the extent of declaring that "His blood be upon us and upon our children" (Matt 27:25). This was a most serious matter according to Jewish law; bloodguilt, or the liability for punishment for shedding blood, attaches to the slayer and his family (II Sam 3:28) for generations (II Kings 9:26), and even to his city (Jer 26:5), nation (Deut 21:8), and land (Deut 24:4). In the case of lawful execution, the blood of the victim remains on his own person, but innocent blood cries out for vengeance (Gen 4:10), is rejected by the earth (Isa 26:21; Ezek 24:7), and pollutes it (Num 35:33-34).

One possible conclusion is that the temple priests feared the influence that Jesus maintained over the populace, believing that they would lose political power, tithes, and taxes, but it does not explain why they did not resort to the ordinary means of execution. The Biblical accounts stress that it was the Jews themselves who insisted on crucifying Jesus according to the Roman custom. The letter of Pilate[17] indicates that they were driven by hatred; according to this source, the crucifixion was the action of an angry mob that had lost control. This seems to make far more sense, because crucifixion was so terrible that it would not have been requested under normal circumstances. While the Romans sometimes crucified Jews, it was highly unusual for the Jews to request this form of death for one of their own people.

The Roman form of crucifixion was always preceded by a scourging at the place of judgment, so merciless that many died from it. The criminal, still unclothed, was then made to carry his cross (the crossbeam or *patibulum*) along the public roads to the execution

---

[17] "Pontius Pilate, Governor of Judea, to Tiberius Caesar, Emperor of Rome." *Archaeological Writings of the Sanhedrin and Talmuds of the Jews*. Trans. by Dr. McIntosh and Twyman. (St. Louis, MO: Rev. W. D. Mahan and Eld. J. W. Damon, 1887).

ground, as a warning to others. This crossbeam was placed on the back of the victim, across the shoulders, and was often tied to the arms, which made it difficult to walk. Falls were common, and tradition maintains that Jesus fell three times. Because the arms were not free, it was not unusual for the victim to fall on his face. Studies on the Shroud of Turin and the Sudarium Oviedo indicate a greater degree of dirt in the area of the nose and mouth, as well a nose that was flattened to the right. This indicates that the person indeed fell, and in the case of Jesus, the third fall has always been portrayed in this manner. The *patibulum* weighed about 110 pounds and would have required a great effort to carry it, especially for a man who had been subjected to a severe scourging with considerable loss of blood.

A *titulus*, or placard, was placed at the top of the upright stake, and was generally worn around the neck of the victim as he walked to the place of death. Bearing the reason for execution, it was written in three languages: Aramaic, the vernacular; Greek, the language of the Roman world; and Latin, the language of the Roman administration. The *titulus* given to Jesus by Pilate contained the title "King of the Jews" (Mt 27:37; Mk 15:26; Lk 23:38; Jn 19:19-22). If nailed, the victim was fastened first to the crossbeam while he was still on the ground, with spikes through the base of the palm of the hand in the wrist area; he was then elevated together with the crossbeam to the upright beam, and was secured to it with nails through the feet or above the heels. Death occurred as the result of asphyxiation and heart failure, caused because the weight of the body prevented the functioning of the lung muscles.

According to Santiago Santidrián Alegre, physiologist at the University of Navarra, there are many factors that contribute to the death of a crucifixion victim: a) Enormous emotional tension and intense discharge of adrenaline that endangers the physiology of the skin and the heart, b) Shock produced by the loss of blood, c) Heart failure with pulmonary edema, which progressively aggravates the ability to breathe, d) Malfunction of the kidneys, e) Increase in urea with serious pressure on the central nervous system, f) Respiratory acidosis with hyperventilation and an effect on the nerves, and g) Circulatory clots that can damage vital organs, especially the heart. The studies of EDICES on the Sudarium of Oviedo and the Shroud of

Turin show that the first cause of death was asphyxiation from pulmonary edema, but that Jesus also suffered from a high fever and an excess of acid in the blood. He was dehydrated by the intense sweating and suffered continuous cramps, as well as chills and fits of shivering. In the judgment of the investigators, the fever is what justifies the cadaveric rigidity that is noticeable on the Holy Shroud[18].

Jesus was crucified at the hands of the Roman authorities, when "Pontius Pilate was governor of Judea, and Herod was tetrarch of Galilee" (Lk 3:1). He was brought before Pilate by the Sanhedrin, who brought charges against him, among them that he claimed to be the Messiah (Lk 23:1-5). Crucifixion was not a Jewish custom, and therefore Jesus was taken to Pilate in order to induce the governor to nail him to the cross as a rebel in the estimation of Rome. The Biblical account of the execution of Jesus agrees with the Roman method of execution, but there were, however, several concessions made because of Jewish custom: a) Jesus was given back his clothes after being scourged (Mk 15:20; Mt 27:31), b) He was given aid in carrying the cross (Mk 15:21), c) He was offered a drink of spiced wine which He refused (Mk 15:23; Mt 27:34), and d) Contrary to the Roman practice of leaving the body on the cross for days as a sign of disgrace and as a warning to others, that of Jesus was removed and buried before sunset of the same day, in accordance with Jewish law (Dt 21:23; Mk 15:42).

The Romans raised Jesus on a fairly high stake, so that He could be seen by everyone, as was their custom with more notorious criminals. When the soldiers tried to put a sponge soaked in wine to his lips, they had to put it on the end of a stick (Mk 15:26; Mt 27:48; Jn 19:29). There were two different heights for the cross: the *crux humilis,* which allowed the wild beasts in the area to attack the crucified easily, and the *crux sublimis,* reserved for those whom it was especially desirable to display.

An interesting document, previously referred to, is found in the *Archaeological Writings of the Sanhedrin and Talmuds of the Jews,* translated from manuscripts in Constantinople and the records of the senatorial docket taken from the Vatican in Rome. This is the letter of Pontius

---

[18] Alfons García, from an article published in *LINTEUM 24-25.*

Pilate, Governor of Judea, to Tiberius Caesar, Emperor of Rome, supposedly written only a few days after the death of Jesus. One might doubt its authenticity with good reason, but it does not appear to contradict the Bible in any way, and seems to clarify to some extent some of the reasons for Jesus' crucifixion. Pilate affirms that he did not believe that Jesus intended to stir up the people against the Romans, although he was apprehensive at first, because Jesus spoke more as a friend of the Romans than the Jews. On account of the wisdom of his sayings Pilate granted a great deal of liberty to the Nazarene, for it was in his power to have had him arrested and exiled. Rather, Pilate extended to him his protection; Jesus "was at liberty to act, to speak, to assemble and address the people, to choose disciples, unrestrained by any praetorian mandate." This unlimited freedom, however, provoked the Jews, not the poor, but the rich and powerful, who made complaints daily at the praetorium and insisted that if the praetor refused justice, an appeal would be made to Caesar. Pilate requested an interview with Jesus, and warned him of the hatred of his enemies. Jesus calmly replied that Pilate was incapable of stopping the torrent of events; it was inevitable that the blood of the just be spilt, and was not in his power to arrest the victim at the foot of the tabernacle of expiation.

On the day of the crucifixion, the city was overflowing with a tumultuous populace, clamoring for the death of Jesus, composed primarily of the three powerful parties that had joined forces against him: the Herodians, the Sadducees, and the Pharisees. After the High Priest condemned him to death, Caiaphas sent Jesus to Pilate to secure the execution. Pilate answered that, as Jesus was a Galilean, the affair fell under Herod's jurisdiction, and ordered him to be sent there, but Herod committed the fate of Jesus to Pilate. Pilate told the people that Roman justice does not punish blasphemy, the crime for which Jesus had been charged, with death. He argued that crucifixion was incompatible with Jewish law, because a criminal judge could not pass sentence on a criminal unless he had fasted one whole day. A sentence must have the consent of the Sanhedrin, signed by the president, and no criminal could be executed on the same day he was sentenced. The people refused to listen, so Pilate ordered that Jesus be scourged, hoping that it would satisfy them, but it only increased their fury. He then washed his hands in the presence of the multitude.

According to the letter of Pilate, nothing could be compared to what he witnessed on that occasion: it was as if "all the phantoms of the infernal regions had assembled at Jerusalem." The day had darkened "like a winter's twilight, such as had been at the death of the great Julius Caesar." The signs seen both in the heavens and on the earth were so dreadful that Dionysius the Areopagite is reported to have exclaimed, "Either the author of nature is suffering, or the universe is falling apart." A dreadful earthquake filled everyone with fear and especially frightened the Jews. After the death of Jesus, the crowd returned home, gloomy, taciturn and desperate, because what they had witnessed had stricken them with terror and remorse. Joseph of Arimathea came to him for permission to bury Jesus, and Pilate ordered Manlius to take some soldiers with him to superintend the interment, lest it should be profaned. A few days later the sepulcher was found empty, and the disciples were saying that Jesus had risen from the dead, as he had foretold. Pilate affirms that he had ordered Malcus, the captain of the royal guard to place as many Jewish soldiers around the sepulcher as were needed, so that if anything should happen they would blame themselves, and not the Romans. This was indeed carried out; Malcus confirmed that he had placed his lieutenant, Ben Isham, with one hundred soldiers around the sepulcher. The penalty for them to sleep on duty was death. After the body was reported missing, the priests interrogated the soldiers, who affirmed that they had not been asleep, and had not seen the disciples. Many thought that Jesus was not a human being. The letter concludes as follows:

> He could convert water into wine; he could change death into life, diseases into health; he could calm the seas, still the storms, call up fish with a silver coin in his mouth. Now, I say, if he could do all these things – which he did, and many more, as the Jews all testify; and it was doing these things that created this enmity against him; he was not charged with criminal offenses, nor was he charged with violating any law, nor of wronging any individual in person; all these facts are known to thousands, as well by his foes as by his friends; so I am almost ready to say, as did Manulas at the cross, "Truly this was the Son of God."

The Descent from the Cross

The Sudarium of Oviedo indicates that after death, a mixture of blood and water began to flow from the nose and mouth after death had occurred. The cloth would have remained in position for about an hour while the body was still in a vertical position on the cross, and the position of the head and the right arm prevented the cloth from wrapping the head completely. This is perfectly compatible with the death of Jesus because it would have taken some time to obtain the necessary permission from Pilate to remove the body; nevertheless, this cloth was necessary to contain the flow of blood in order to prevent it from being lost. As previously mentioned, it was thought that the blood contained the soul of the person, and the hand prints on the Sudarium indicate that someone tried to contain the flow of blood.

From studies done on the Shroud of Turin, it is certain that the body of Christ was carried horizontally to the tomb, but that it was not until then that it was placed on the shroud. The Shroud contains only the impression of the clots of blood formed on the skin of the back during the journey to the tomb; therefore, the greater part of the blood was lost at some point prior to when the body was wrapped in the shroud. It appears that, according to tradition, the body was carried to the tomb wrapped in some sort of cloth. This is also supported by Jewish custom, because beliefs about the importance of the blood would not have allowed that it be permitted to flow into the earth. This second shroud could correspond to the cloth seen by Arculf in Jerusalem in the second half of the seventh century, which was possibly later destroyed in the French Revolution. All the Gospels mention that Jesus was wrapped in a *clean* shroud, which is an indication that there were two. For the same reasons of decency that demanded that the head of Jesus be covered, it is unthinkable that the body would not have been likewise wrapped in a cloth during the journey to the tomb. Some believe that this shroud would have covered the head as well, but the Sudarium of Oviedo indicates otherwise. A large cloth could not have wrapped the head in the same manner as did the Sudarium, and this would have been necessary in order to contain the blood flow.

Studies on the Sudarium of Oviedo have shown that the body was left on the cross for approximately two hours. The rigidity of the corpse would be extreme, fixed in the position of crucifixion. Victims of this form of punishment were taken down in the same manner in which they were lifted to the cross. The feet were first freed by drawing out the nails, the *patibulum* was lowered with the body still rigid and attached, and the body and crossbeam were then lowered to the ground. Pierre Barbet believes that five bearers were necessary to remove the body, still attached to the *patibulum,* from the vertical piece of wood, or *stipes,* because they had to carry a body weighing approximately 176 lbs. and the heavy crossbeam, at least another 110 lbs. It is likely that a preliminary shroud was also used at this point, in order to prevent more blood from spilling into the earth. At this point the nails were removed, and the arms were brought back from their outstretched position. Barbet testifies that this would still be possible in spite of the *post mortem* rigidity. The Sudarium was re-wrapped around the head in preparation for the transport of the body to the tomb, and the body would have been prepared in a similar manner. Scientific studies indicate that this interim period lasted about one hour, a sufficient amount of time to carry out these procedures. A preliminary anointing would also have been possible during this period, and the body would then have been transported to the tomb, with a number of bearers holding the body on the outer side.

While the Gospels only mention that Joseph of Arimathea took the body to the tomb, there had to have been a number of bearers. Studies on the Sudarium of Oviedo show that one person kept his left hand over the cloth that covered the face in an attempt to contain the blood flow, and several more men were necessary to carry the body. Jewish burial tradition demanded that relatives and close friends also accompany the procession to mourn the deceased; therefore, Mary, the mother of Jesus, the Apostle John, and the women present at the foot of the cross during the crucifixion would have also escorted the body.

Burial

The proper interment of the dead was an important matter for the Jews, and took place on the day of death based on the law in Deuteronomy 21:23; from this the rabbinical interpretation derived from it is that "no corpse is to remain unburied overnight"[19]. This was done for reasons of sanitation and fear of defilement (Num. 19:11-14), and also because of the climate and the fact that the Israelites did not embalm the dead. According to Rebecca Jackson, "the rush to inter the body of the deceased is innate within the Jewish mentality," and the deceased continue to be buried as soon as possible after death, even today when it is no longer necessary. The thought of lying unburied was abhorrent and can be measured by the frequency with which the Bible refers to this fear. The importance of burial can also be seen in the considerable care that was taken in hewing out the tombs of the Israelite period in Palestine. Caves were often purchased as a family tomb, as was the case with Abraham (Gen. 23).

According to *The Jewish Encyclopedia,* the tomb was not immediately closed. For the first three days it was the custom for relatives to visit the grave to see whether the deceased had come back to life, because "quick burials involved the danger of entombing persons alive[20]." In the case of Jesus, a stone was rolled against the entrance to the tomb and it was "secured until the third day" (Mt 27:64), for fear that the disciples would steal the body and proclaim that He had risen from the dead. Nevertheless, the appearance of the women at the tomb on Sunday morning to anoint the body one last time can be considered to be quite normal and within the three-day period. Mark 16:1 is often interpreted as a sign that the burial had not been complete, but as already discussed, a second anointing was a common expression of respect, and none of the evangelists have written that the women were there to wash the body because it had been improperly interred.

Coffins were not generally used in Biblical times. The dead were carried to the place of burial on a bier, accompanied by flautists and mourners who eulogized the deceased with their laments, gestures, tears, and cries of grief. Those who transported the deceased had to go without shoes for the duration of the procession. The procession varied greatly according to the importance of the person and the circumstances of death. Josephus describes the elaborate procession of Herod, who was taken to Herodium to be buried:

---

[19] Sanh. vi. 4, 46a; Maimonides, "Abel," iv. 8 et al., *The Jewish Encyclopedia,* Op. Cit., p. 432.

[20] *The Jewish Encyclopedia,* "Burial," p. 434.

The body was carried upon a golden bier, embroidered with very precious stones of great variety, and it was covered over with purple, as well as the body itself: he had a diadem upon his head, and above it a crown of gold: he also had a scepter in his right hand. (198) About the bier were his sons and his numerous relations; next to these was the soldiers, distinguished according to their several countries and ranks; and they were put into the following order: First of all went his guards, then the band of Thracians, and after them the Germans; and next the band of Galatians, everyone in their full war attire; and behind these marched the whole army in the same manner as they used to go out to war, (199) and as they used to be put in array by the masters of the roll call and centurions; these were followed by five hundred of his servants carrying spices.[21]

In stark contrast to that of King Herod, the procession of Jesus was quite simple, with the body transported to the nearby garden tomb of Joseph of Arimathea, a "new tomb where no one had ever been laid" (Jn 19:38-42). Studies on the Sudarium show that this procession lasted no more than five or ten minutes, which would be the amount of time required to carry a body from the traditional site of Golgotha in the Church of the Holy Sepulcher in Jerusalem, to the nearby tomb, now a separate chapel in the same church.

While some may question whether or not John and Mary, the mother of Jesus, accompanied the burial procession to the tomb, Jewish custom indicates that this almost certainly would have been the case. It was considered to be extremely important for family, relatives, and close friends to accompany the body to the tomb under normal circumstances; the only exception would be in the case of the high priest, who was not permitted to have contact with the dead under any circumstances. Furthermore, John's presence would have been required to help transport the body.

Criminals, however, were another matter. It was required that convicts executed by order of the Jewish court be interred in a cemetery set aside for that special purpose, known as the court's graveyard. According to the law, private persons were not allowed to

---

[21] *Jewish Antiquities*, Book 17, Ch. 8, no. 3.

bury such convicts, and no one was permitted to mourn them. On the other hand, convicts executed by order of the Roman governor had to be buried and mourned like any person who had died a natural death. Because Jesus was sentenced to death by a Roman court, he was entitled to the benefits of Jewish burial and traditional Jewish mourning. The Bible specifically mentions that Mary Magdalene and the other Mary remained at the tomb after the stone had been rolled in front of the entrance (Mt 27:61; Mk 15:47). While nothing is said about the others, traditional mourning ritual would have required the presence of all those who had been present at the foot of the cross. It is impossible to believe that the beloved disciple and the mother of Jesus would not have been present at the tomb, not only because this was essential according to Jewish law and tradition, but also because they were the two people who were closest to Jesus. One can be certain beyond a reasonable doubt, therefore, that John was an eyewitness of the burial. He would have known where the sudarium was placed in the tomb on Friday, and his Gospel account can be considered to be an affirmation of the fact that the cloth had not been moved from the position in which it had been placed on Friday afternoon.

The necropolises of first-century Palestine were outside of the cities, which can easily be verified in Jerusalem today when one observes the tombs that surround the city, particularly to the east, south and north. The tombs were at times excavated in a plot, garden or orchard, but family sepulchers were also common, because for the ancient Hebrews to die was "to be gathered unto his people" and "to lie with his fathers" (Gen 49:29; Num 27:13; Jud 2:10). The cave of Makpelah thus became the family tomb of the Patriarchs (Gen 23, 49:29-31). These tombs were either dug out of the ground close to the dwelling place of the family, or were hewn out of the rock of a cave[22].

In the first centuries before and after Christ it was especially common for families with the economic means to excavate their sepulchral monuments in the rocks, and this was generally accomplished in the rocky hillsides close to the population (Mt 27:60). This type of tomb was normally composed of two fairly square

---

[22] *The Jewish Encyclopedia*, Op. Cit., p. 436-7.

chambers, joined by a very narrow and low opening, sufficient to allow the passage of a person bending down. The sepulchral chamber was the one that was farthest from the entrance, which contained niches distributed along the lateral and back walls[23]. The antechamber had flat walls and a continuous bench excavated in the rock along the walls. The shrouding ritual was often performed here, especially in the case of those who had died in a tragic manner or were executed, as well as any other last details. The normal position of the body was horizontal and face upward. To be buried without garments was considered a disgrace, but burying the dead in costly, extravagant garments was also frowned upon. Simple linen garments were preferred.

In the case of Jesus, much is made of the fact that the body wasn't washed, and that the Sudarium was removed from the face before the body was wrapped in a clean linen shroud, but these procedures were quite normal, as already explained. The Sudarium appears to have been used during the descent from the cross and the procession to the tomb. Its function was to contain the blood that flowed from the nose and the mouth after death, as well as to cover the disfigured face of Jesus from public view. For reasons of uncleanness, it would have been removed before the body was wrapped in a clean shroud, and placed in a separate place in the tomb because of the large amount of blood it contained. Although it is quite probable that the burial rituals were hastened in the case of Jesus because of the shortage of time, there is no reason to believe that they were incomplete or not in compliance with the law. The law, while it did require the use of a chin band, which is indicated in the case of Jesus, did not require the placement of a sudarium beneath the shroud, in the sense of a cloth like the Sudarium of Oviedo that completely wrapped the head. Jewish burial procedures also exempted those who had lost blood during death from the washing ritual. The reason, once again, is that the blood was considered to be a sacred part of the body that should also be interred.

According to *The Encyclopedia Judaica*, it was prescribed in post-talmudic times, in the case of the victim of an unnatural death, that he be buried in his blood-soaked garments over which the white shrouds

---

[23] Florentino Díez, "Ritos funerarios judíos en la Palestina del Siglo I."

were placed, in "order that all parts of the body should be interred[24]."
The Code of Jewish Law from the sixteenth century even states:

> *If a person falls and dies instantly, if his body was bruised and blood flowed from the wound, and there is apprehension that his life-blood was absorbed in his clothes, he should not be ritually cleansed, but interred in his garments and shoes. He should be wrapped in a sheet, above his garments. That sheet is called sobeb. It is customary to scoop up the earth at the spot where he fell, and if blood happens to be there or near by, all that earth is buried with him[25].*

The tradition that Mary Magdalene returned to the scene of the Crucifixion to dig up the earth that had been soaked with the blood of Jesus is well known, but generally not taken seriously because it is foreign to our way of thinking. It is fascinating, however, that the Monastery of St. Toribio in Liébana lists in its inventory of relics, "a great part of the Blood and Water that flowed from the Side of Christ, collected by St. Mary Magdalene at the foot of the Cross." According to Jewish law, this would not have been the overtly pious and excessively sentimental act of a woman, but necessary. It must be pointed out, however, that the anointing procedure was essential to the burial ritual, and after the death of Jesus this was indeed carried out at the tomb of Joseph of Arimathea. The ritual of the first burial normally ended with a banquet, sometimes celebrated in the atrium or vestibule of the monumental tombs, but due to the scarcity of time would not have taken place in the case of Jesus. This custom, however, indicates that Mary, the mother of Jesus, John the Apostle, and the other women were indeed present at the tomb during the burial of Jesus. Family and friends stayed with the deceased until the last moment.

Although a corpse was considered to be the ultimate category of defilement, the need to bury the dead took precedence over this fear. Individuals who had been defiled through contact with the dead were

---

[24] *Encyclopedia Judaica*, "Burial," p. 1519.

[25] Cited by Gilbert R. Lavoie, *Unlocking the Secrets of the Shroud* (Allen, Texas: Thomas More, 1998).

purified during a seven-day period that included immersion in a specially prepared pool of water. No one made unclean by contact with a dead body could celebrate the Passover, however, for the first month; those who buried Jesus, therefore, would not have been permitted to celebrate this feast. Priests could only bury members of their immediate family (Ezek 44:25), and the high priest and the Nazarites could not contaminate themselves even for their parents (Lev 21:11; Num 6:7)[26].

The body normally remained in the tomb for a period of one year, or until only the bones remained. Expiation was achieved through decay of the flesh, which was believed to contain the sins of the individual. The bones were considered to be pure, and were then placed in ossuaries, which are stone jars used for this purpose.

---

[26] *The Interpreter's Dictionary of the Bible* (Nashville: Abingdon Press, 1962): Vol. 1, p. 644.

CHAPTER ELEVEN

DATING
THE CRUCIFIXION

D ating the Crucifixion of Jesus has been a difficult matter, but the majority of scholars are of the opinion that it could have taken place in one of two years: AD 30 or AD 33. We know, first of all, that Christ was crucified when Pontius Pilate was the Roman ruler of Judea, which was between the years 26 and 36 AD. We also know that it was a Friday, according to the Gospels. One of the problems has been that there is a discrepancy between the synoptic Gospels and the Gospel of John. Matthew, Mark and Luke infer that Friday was the 15th of Nisan, or the day of Passover, while John affirms that Friday was the 14th of Nisan, or the day before Passover. Some have suggested that John altered the date in order to connect the death of Jesus with the killing of the Passover lambs, and others argue that Matthew, Mark, and Luke altered the date in order to establish the Eucharist as the Christian Passover. There are, however, several important considerations for the validity of John's date: a) According to *The Jewish Encyclopedia,* an execution could not have been held on the day of the Passover, b) It has been suggested that Matthew's date could easily be the result of a mistranslation from the original Hebrew, c) Matthew, Mark, and Luke do not explicitly state the date, and d) John is supported by two passages of the Talmud. One places the death of Jesus on the 14th of Nisan, and the other places the Passover amnesty of Barabbas on the eve of the Passover, the 14th of Nisan. According to astronomical calculations, the 14th of Nisan fell on a Friday only twice between the years 26 and 36 AD: the years 30 and 33.

Two scientists from the University of Oxford in Great Britain, Colin J. Humphreys and W. G. Waddington, published the most detailed study to date on the astronomical data that can help determine the day and year of the Crucifixion. Their study was published in the magazine *Nature,* vol. 306, December 22-29, 1983, and a summary written by Dr. Manuel M. Carreira, S.J. of the University of Cleveland was subsequently published in *LINTEUM,* the publication of CES. According to them, the exact day and year can be calculated with precision. Their arguments and conclusions will be summarized here.

First of all, it is necessary to remember how the day of Passover was calculated in the Jewish calendar, and how the beginning of each day was established with respect to the apparent movement of the Sun. The Hebrew month was the lunar month, with 29.5 days. There were 11 days left over at the end of the year, which meant that it was necessary to add one more month approximately every three years. This was done if the normal calculation of Passover placed it before the beginning of spring (March 21), or if excessive cold delayed the harvesting of the first fruits that had to be presented on the day of Passover.

The lunar month began with the first indication of the New Moon, hardly visible at sunset. Two weeks later, when the 14th of Nisan ended with the Full Moon, Passover was celebrated. Astronomical calculations based on the latitude of Jerusalem, in recent observations of the New Moon, and in the presupposition of an atmosphere of normal transparency, give us the dates and hours of the New Moon during the years 26 to 36. During these years, the 14th of Nisan occurred on a Friday in the years 30 (April 7, possibly the 6, if there were abnormal atmospheric conditions), 33 (April 3), and 27 (April 10, possibly the 11th for the same reason).

According to these scientists, the year 27 is too soon, because John the Baptist began his preaching in the year 15 of Tiberius Caesar, which corresponds to autumn of 28-29, according to the Roman civil calendar, or spring of 29-30 in the Jewish ecclesiastical calendar. The baptism of Jesus by John was the beginning of his public life, and if we add two or three years to the earliest date possible, the 28th, we are already in the year 30.

Thus there are two possible dates for the 14th of Nisan: Friday, the 7th of April of the year 30, or Friday, the 3rd of April of the year 33. In both cases the Crucifixion occurs the day before Passover and before Saturday, as John indicates, which also coincides with Jewish prescription against executions on the feast of the Passover and the Sabbath. The Last Supper, therefore, was not a Passover meal celebrated on the official date, and Christ died on the cross while the Paschal lambs were being sacrificed, on the afternoon of the 14th of Nisan.

Because of the calculation that the beginning of the public ministry could not have been before the year 28, and because St. John mentions three Passovers, including that of the Crucifixion, the year 30 is unacceptable. The authors add one more fact that reinforces all of the arguments that point to the 3rd of April of the year 33 as the only acceptable date.

In his Pentecostal discourse to people congregated in the cenacle, St. Peter, surrounded by the Apostles, who were speaking in multiple tongues after receiving the Spirit, refutes the accusation of being intoxicated, appealing to the fulfillment of a prophesy: "This is what was spoken through the prophet Joel: 'It will come to pass in the last days,' God says, 'that I will pour out a portion of my spirit upon all flesh.... And I will work wonders in the heavens above and signs on the earth below... The sun shall be turned to darkness, and the moon to blood, before the coming of the great and splendid day of the Lord" (Acts 2:16-20).

Given the supernatural sense of astronomical phenomena in the ancient conception of the cosmos, it is plausible that Peter interpreted as significant any unusual aspect of the Sun or the Moon on the day of the Crucifixion. According to Matthew (27:45), while Christ was dying on the Cross there was a period of three hours of darkness: The Sun "turned to darkness," not because of a solar eclipse, which was impossible with a Full Moon, but very probably because of a sandstorm.

Peter may also be referring to a real and recent observation when he says that the prophecy was fulfilled concerning the Moon "turning to blood." This can be attributed to a phenomenon that is very well-known in lunar eclipses: the part of the Moon immersed in the shadow of the Earth frequently acquires a red color because it receives light refracted by the terrestrial atmosphere, with characteristics similar to the light of dawn or of sunset. What Peter says, therefore, is surprisingly accurate, because the 14th of Nisan of the year 33, on April 3rd of our calendar, there was a partial eclipse of the Moon visible in Jerusalem precisely when the Moon was coming out, and while the Sun was setting. Only in the year 33 did this coincidence occur, that on the 14th of Nisan the paschal Moon appeared eclipsed when observed in Jerusalem, with 20% of its disc a red color. The eclipse ended a half hour later, at 6:50 in the afternoon, leaving the Full Moon in all of the splendor that was characteristic of Passover.

Concerning the date of Jesus' birth, which is no less debated than the year of his death, experts are only able to say with certainty that it must have occurred at some time between 7 BC and 7 AD. Nevertheless, because we know that Jesus was about thirty years of age when he began his public ministry (Lk 3:23), and the year 33 AD is the last acceptable date for the death of Jesus according to most scholars, these dates can be narrowed down considerably. Most believe that his life must fall completely between the death of Herod in 4 BC and the year 33 AD, and it is not likely that Jesus was born later than the first year of the Christian era. The tradition that Jesus was 33 years of age at the time of the crucifixion is based on nothing more than adding three years to Luke's approximation of his age at the start of his ministry, and a few years more or less would be totally acceptable within the Gospel tradition. If, as some firmly believe, the date of the birth of Jesus is several years before the beginning of the Christian era, the date of 33 AD presents neither an exegetical problem nor an historical one because the imprecise estimation of age given by Luke is not based on documents or official confirmations. It must be remembered, however, that the date of Jesus' birth has never been determined with certainty. It is quite possible that he was exactly 33 years of age when he died.

Concerning the intervals of time indicated by the scientific studies of the Sudarium of Oviedo and the circumstances of that day, EDICES has done an experimental study of the computation of time, comparing what would be necessary in order to form bloodstains similar to those that exist on the Sudarium.

It is known from the Biblical accounts that Jesus was crucified at noon and died at 3:00 p.m. It has already been said that the linen of Oviedo would have been placed on his body when he had been dead for one hour, or around 4:00 p.m. Scientific studies have shown that it took about one hour for the principal stains to be formed, while the body was still on the cross, which means that the body remained there until about

5:00 p.m. This is approximately the amount of time that Joseph of Arimathea would have taken to go to Jerusalem from Golgotha in order to obtain the permission of Pilate to take the body. The body was then placed in a horizontal position on the ground for approximately one more hour, or until about 6:00 p.m. Crucifixion victims were generally taken down the way they were placed on the cross, meaning that Jesus would have been laid on the ground with His arms still nailed to the horizontal bar. The body would have been placed nearly face down, as studies on the Sudarium indicate, with the crossbeam on top. The nails would have been removed, a first anointing may have been carried out, and the body would have been prepared for the transfer to the tomb.

As studies have indicated, the Sudarium was removed from the head at this point and re-wrapped so that it completely surrounded the head, indicating that the right arm that had previously prevented that process could now be moved and repositioned. The body was then taken to another location in less than 10 minutes, according to EDICES. The tomb in the Basilica of the Holy Sepulcher in Jerusalem is about 40 meters from Golgotha, a distance that can easily be covered in this amount of time.

As the astronomical studies of Humphreys and Waddington indicate, on the 3rd of April of the year 33 the moon came out, literally "tinged with blood," at 6:20, as mentioned in the *Acts of the Apostles,* or just as the shrouding process was beginning. The Passover began at approximately 7:15, and therefore there was very little time to complete the ritual once they had arrived at the tomb. In accordance with Jewish custom, the body would not have been washed, but rather heavily anointed with spices and wrapped in a clean shroud. The Sudarium was removed, due to the large amount of blood it contained, was anointed with aloes and myrrh, and was placed in a separate place in the tomb. Other physical remains of His blood would also have been left in the sepulcher, such as blood-soaked earth and any other cloths that may have been used during the transport of the body to the garden tomb of Joseph of Arimathea.

It is, of course, quite likely that there were other linens used during the transport of the body of Jesus to the tomb and His burial. Once again, Shroud studies indicate the use of a chin band, which was placed underneath the shroud; there is also the possibility that linen strips were used, bound to the hands and feet for carrying, as well as a second shroud. When John refers to the *othonia* in the tomb in 20:5-9, he is referring to all of the burial linens, in a general sense. These would include the shroud or shrouds, linen strips and bandages, the chin band, and the sudarium.

PART FOUR

THE SUDARIUM
AND JOHN 20:5-8

So Peter and the other disciple went out and came to the tomb.
They both ran, but the other disciple ran faster than Peter and
arrived at the tomb first; He bent down and saw the burial cloths
there, but did not go in. When Simon Peter arrived after him, he
went into the tomb and saw the burial cloths there, and the cloth
that had covered his head, not with the burial cloths but rolled up
in a separate place. Then the other disciple also went in, the one
who had arrived at the tomb first, and he saw and believed.

JOHN 20:3-8

CHAPTER TWELVE

THE ORIGIN AND MEANING OF THE WORD **SUDARIUM**

John 20:5-8 is possibly one of the most debated Biblical passages, due to the polemics it raises: Exactly what is John referring to when he speaks of the burial cloths in the tomb? Why does their position in the tomb lead the Apostle to faith in the Resurrection? Is the Sudarium of Oviedo the same cloth mentioned by John, and if so, can the recent scientific studies of EDICES help clarify the meaning of the Gospel? The interpretations of this well-known passage are numerous, as well as conflicting, and it indeed appears that the Sudarium of Oviedo can shed some light on the darkness of the empty tomb, dispelling in the process some of the unfounded theories that have arisen concerning its usage.

First of all, it must be mentioned that the Sudarium of Oviedo has always been identified as the *Sudarium Domini,* the Sudarium of the Lord. The title comes from its ancient tradition, and was engraved by King Alfonso II in the silver plating of the chest of relics, in spite of the fact that little had been known historically about the sudarium mentioned by John as being in the tomb of Jesus. Secondly, the *only* Biblical reference to the Sudarium of Jesus is found in this same Gospel of John (Jn 20:6-7). Therefore, it is necessary to question the origin of the word itself. What exactly *is* a sudarium? Two of those whose papers were presented at the First International Congress on the Sudarium of Oviedo have extensively studied the origin and meaning of the word. The first is Enrique López Fernández, Canon of the Cathedral of Oviedo and Professor of Latin and Holy Scripture. The second is Luis García García, Doctor of Theology, Oviedo, Spain.

Enrique López Fernández, in his article entitled *"Juan 20, 5-9. Traducciones e interpretación,"* discusses the problem raised by the mention of the "sudarium" in John 20:7 for the critical investigator. Apart from the fact that the synoptic Gospels do not mention it at all, the Evangelist John does not mention the sudarium during his narration about the tomb (Jn 19:38-42), nor when the beloved Disciple arrives at the tomb, bends down, and looks inside. It is only when Peter arrives after him and goes into the tomb that he sees "the burial cloths there, and the cloth that had covered his head, not with the burial cloths but rolled up in a separate place" (Jn 20:6-7). The presence of the sudarium in the tomb is, of course, not the mere product of the imagination of the evangelist, but the matter of an article that really existed, mentioned perhaps because it was useful to the writer because of the symbolism that he felt it could represent or that historically it had already indeed represented. The fact that it had not been part of the shrouding process would explain why the author had not mentioned it previously.

Most scholars believe that the word *soudárion* spoken of in the text of John is the simple transcription to Greek of the Latin word *sudarium*, a word derived from *sudor,* (to sweat), which clearly alludes to the original function of the article, which was no other than that of wiping sweat from the face. Therefore, it is clear that the sudarium was a fairly small cloth, the equivalent more or less of a large handkerchief, or perhaps napkin or towel, and had nothing to do with the *sindon* or shroud, of the synoptic Gospels.

Others, however, believe that the Johannine *soudárion*, far from being derived from the Latin *sudarium*, is rather the transcription of the Hebrew word *sûdar* or of the Aramaic *sûdera'/sûdara'*, which although it is phonetically similar to the Latin word *sudarium*, has a different meaning. They think that this word can mean a cloth of relatively great proportions, equivalent to a mantle. This opinion, however, does not explain John's insistence that the sudarium "had been on the head of Jesus," because a cloth that would have covered the entire body, as they maintain, could not have been worn on the head. Based on the opinion of S. V. Jastrow, who translates the word as a "scarf wound around the head and hanging down over the neck, turban," López believes that the idea of the Semitic substratum of the sudarium mentioned in the Gospel of John can be accepted, but understood in the sense of a cloth of modest proportions. The

145

sudarium of Jesus could be thus understood as the turban that He was accustomed to wear on His head. This would also clarify the problem that translators have traditionally had when translating this passage of John, who vacillate between the imperfect tense of the original and the past perfect tense demanded by the meaning: "that was/had been on his head."

Luis García García, in his article entitled *"Síndone y Sudario, presentes en la sepultura de Jesús,"* studies the confusion that has always existed between the two words, due to careless translations. Evidence of that confusion can be found in the *Diccionario de la Real Academia Española*. In its three most recent editions (1970, 1978, 1992), the Holy Sudarium, under the entry for *sudario,* is defined as a sheet or linen with which Joseph of Arimathea covered the body of Christ when he lowered him from the cross[1]." Barbet, who also confuses the terms, insists that when St. John wrote *"soudárion"* in Greek, he was referring to the Aramaic *"soudará",* which he believes refers to a full linen garment, which is placed over the head and comes down to the feet. As he explains, "From now onwards, everything becomes quite clear. He found all the linen cloths in the tomb, and among them the shroud rolled up and set apart, which he calls the *"soudárion."* In the course of the centuries the confusion makes itself quite evident, with the word *"sudarium"* often appearing as a synonym for the shroud, as is the case in the account of the pilgrimage of Arçulf.

The two words, however, are never found as synonyms in any Greek dictionary. In the *Greek-English Lexicon*[2], for example, *soudárion* appears with the meaning of *"towel, napkin,"* while *sindón* can even mean *ship's sail,* and is without doubt a cloth of large proportions. In the *Patristic Greek Lexicon,* a *soudárion* is also a cloth of reduced dimensions, according to G. W. LAMPE: *"napkin, towel* worn around head" (...); *"head-cloth* of shroud." In the third meaning given for

---

[1] On the other hand, in *Webster's Encyclopedic Unabridged Dictionary of the English Language* (Random House, 1996), *sudarium* is defined as "(in ancient Rome) a cloth, usually of linen, for wiping the face; handkerchief; and *sindon* as a "cloth of fine linen or silk, used esp. for shrouds."

[2] H. G. Liddell and R. Scott (Oxford University Press, 1992).

sindón, in the Liturgy it means *"linen cloth covering the altar.*[3]*"* It can be concluded, therefore, that the meanings attributed to *soudárion* refer to cloths that never exceed the dimensions of a handkerchief, napkin or towel. The synoptic Gospels expressly say that the "body" of Jesus was wrapped with a cloth (*sindón*), and this clearly exceeds the dimensions of any *soudárion*. A sheet would never be used to wipe sweat from the face.

Sindón appears five times in the New Testament, and *soudárion* four times, according to the statistics of M. Guerra Gómez[4]. Judging by the cases in which they appear, it can be easily concluded that they were very different cloths.

The dimensions of the *sindón* were such that with it the body of the Lord was wrapped, as can be seen in the three synoptic Gospels. St. Mark tells us also that a youth, whom they tried to arrest in Gethsemani, was covered with a *sindon*; but, when they seized him, he left the cloth behind and ran off naked (14:51-52).

On the other hand, a *sudarium* had been wrapped around the head of the diseased Lazarus (Jn 11:44) and covered the head of the dead body of Jesus (Jn 20:7). The dimensions of a *sudarium* are about those of a handkerchief or scarf: they were sufficient to keep in it a silver coin (Lk 19:20). For St. Paul, the *sudaria* that he carried with him were taken to be applied to the sick, so that their diseases would leave them (Acts 19:12). *The New American Bible* translates the word as "face cloths or aprons," and it is quite clear that Paul did not carry "sheets" around with him to touch to the sick.

There is another work that sheds some light on the use of the sudarium, that of Fr. José O'Callaghan, called "The sudarium in the Greek Papyrus of the Roman Times[5]." The author compares the meanings of the words: "sudarium," "facial," and "orarium," each one appearing on a different papyrus. His conclusion is that a "sudarium"

---

[3] García notes that until the subsequent changes of the Second Vatican Council, it was prescribed in the Church that the altar cloths be of linen, because the body of the Lord had been wrapped in such a cloth [Cf. *Catechism Notes* (Dublin: The Anthonian Press, 1964): 115].

[4] *El idioma del Nuevo Testamento* (Burgos 1981): 225-226.

[5] Published in *Archiv für Papyrusforschung* 22/23 (1973): 147-150.

was an article of linen, of common usage for the people of the villages. When printed or embroidered it could serve as a feminine adornment. It could also protect from the cold of winter. In the household, it could be used as a bath towel. It was sometimes imprinted with the name of the locality that specialized in the fabrication of the cloth. The sudarium, therefore, could have many uses: as a towel, sweat cloth, scarf, or turban.

It can be concluded, therefore, that a *soudárion* is never large enough to wrap an entire human body, and that the *sindón* referred to by the three synoptic Gospels is without doubt a completely different cloth. The *sudarium,* according to John, was on the head of Jesus, while the *sindon* wrapped His body.

CHAPTER THIRTEEN

THE SUDARIUM OF JOHN 20

There are two possibilities being discussed today when speaking of the function of the sudarium, according to López Fernández. First, that it is a part of the shroud, and second, that it is a cloth that was used at some moment during the burial process, but that has nothing to do with the shroud. The first is the traditional hypothesis, while the second makes far more sense in the light of the recent studies on the Sudarium of Oviedo.

López Fernández explains that for those who understand that the sudarium was part of the shroud, there are two criteria that influence their point of view: the value attributed to the Greek preposition *epi*, and the parallel case of the burial and shrouding of Lazarus (Jn 11:44). The Greek preposition means "on," and therefore the majority of people opt to understand it as a cloth that served simply to cover the head or the face of Jesus. Those who seek to understand the meaning of the word from the account of the shrouding of Lazarus understand it in the sense of a "chin band," which is a cloth of relatively small dimensions that would have served to tie the jaw of Jesus in order to keep the mouth closed after death. This type of cloth wrapped the entire face below the chin and formed a knot at the top of the head. These options – that the cloth was "on" the head of Jesus, or that it wrapped around his head – are both reflected in the many translations of the Gospel which can be found in circulation. For example, *The New American Bible* translates "that had *covered* his head," which conveys the same meaning as "on," while *Douay-Reims* translates "the napkin that had been *about* his head," suggesting that it had *wrapped* the head.

All of these options imply that the sudarium was part of the shroud, without suspecting that it could have been used at some point during the burial process without having had anything to do with the shrouding itself. The sindonologist Fr. Guilio Ricci was the first to suggest that the

149

sudarium was nothing other than a cloth that for reasons of decency was placed on the face of the deceased when it was especially disfigured, and that the wounded face of Jesus would have been covered at the time of the descent from the cross and during the time when He was being taken to the tomb. It would not have been used in the burial itself, but placed in a separate place.

For López Fernández, it is not likely that the sudarium was part of the shrouding ritual for several reasons. First, it is never mentioned in this sense. The synoptic Gospels say only that they "wrapped Him in a linen shroud," and none of the evangelists mention a sudarium being used during the burial. Secondly, if the sudarium had been part of the shrouding of Jesus, many difficulties arise that are practically irresolvable. If the sudarium had been placed underneath the shroud, as was the case with Lazarus, how would it be possible for Peter and the other disciple to see it? If it were a chin band, it would have been placed beneath the shroud, and would have served no useful purpose, since, by virtue of the *rigor mortis* when Jesus was lowered from the cross, where He had remained with the head inclined on the chest, the mouth could not be open. If the Shroud of Turin is authentic, how could the image pass through the sudarium without leaving an imprint on it, or at least without leaving some indication on the shroud of a linen underneath? If one believes that it was placed on top of the shroud, what function could it possibly have had? Why is John so insistent that the sudarium was in a separate place, and not with the other burial cloths? If the cloth had indeed been rolled up and moved to a separate place, how could this have brought John to faith in the resurrection? On the contrary, it might have convinced him that the body had been stolen.

From the studies that have been carried out on the Sudarium of Oviedo, it has been well documented that the sudarium could be a linen cloth used to wrap the head, instead of being on the head. It is also likely that it was a common cloth, as demonstrated by EDICES, and not the more expensive type of linen used to wrap the bodies of the deceased. With these observations they believe it is possible to formulate a new "reading" of the Johannine Gospel, in order to clarify how the Sudarium was placed. The scientific investigations lead one to exclude the two hypotheses that it was placed on top of the Holy Shroud, in a non-ritualistic way, or that it would have been placed in contact with the face, with the Shroud placed over it. According to García, when Simon Peter entered the tomb and saw the cloth that had covered his head, not with the other burial cloths, but rolled up in a separate place, the meaning of the Greek verb *"entylisso,"* in the perfect passive participle, now clarifies the series of events. The sudarium was positioned and placed apart during the burial process, and was found later, still in the same place as before.

García's studies show that the Sudarium of Oviedo had to have been used before wrapping the body in any other linen, particularly in the Shroud of Turin. The image of the face on the Shroud of Turin, as well as that of the lateral surface of the head, negates the possibility that this person had another linen placed around his head. The stains of blood on the Sudarium of Oviedo also point in the same direction. The sudarium therefore, was not part of the shrouding process. It was used during the descent from the cross and during the transport of the body to the tomb, in order to cover the disfigured face of Jesus, according to the orders of the Sanhedrin, and to prevent loss of blood. It was then removed and placed separately in the tomb. John 20:7 also indicates that Jesus had the Sudarium placed on his head before the burial, but not after. It would have been necessary to remove the cloth in order to anoint the facial wounds, and would not have been used to cover the face once again due to the large amount of blood it contained. It was sufficient to wrap the body in a clean white linen shroud, and is unthinkable that a dirty, bloodstained linen would have left in place on the head of Jesus. While Jewish burial customs would have exempted Jesus from the washing ritual, a clean shroud was required by law.

It is possible to make the following conclusions, according to Guillermo Heras Moreno and José Delfín Villalaín Blanco, members of EDICES[6]:

1. The word "sudarium," derived from the Greek *soudárion,* is a linen used to wipe the sweat from the face, about the size of a towel, scarf,

---

[6] "El Sudario de Oviedo: ¿Envolvió la cabeza de Jesús? Discrepancias con la Síndone de Turín," *El Sudario de Oviedo: Hallazgos recientes* (Valencia, 1998).

or a small tablecloth. It can never be understood as a synonym for shroud. It might also be associated with a turban. It is quite possible that a common cloth of this size would have had multiple uses, and it is not unreasonable to think that one of Jesus' friends or relatives, present at the crucifixion, would have had His turban in their possession and lent it to Joseph of Arimathea and Nicodemus as they were taking Jesus from the cross.

2. If one compares the mention of the sudarium made in John 20:7 with the linen mentioned in John 11:44 in the narration of the raising of Lazarus, it can be said that the sudarium was a mortuary linen that wrapped the head of the diseased, normally before the shroud was placed on the body.

3. According to the synoptic Gospels, the body of Jesus was wrapped in a shroud. It would serve no purpose to wrap the head in a sudarium on top of the shroud.

4. It is logical to think that the sudarium that wrapped the head of Jesus was used before wrapping his body in the shroud, and that it was then taken from him and deposited in the sepulcher in a place where it was visible upon entering. This is supported by the Gospel accounts, due to the fact that it was stained with life blood and had to be anointed with aloes and myrrh, and that it would have thus served a logical function in the burial process.

5. According to the norms of the Sanhedrin, when the face of an executed man is deformed it must be covered with a linen. This agrees perfectly with the use of the Sudarium that has been determined by EDICES: that the cloth wrapped the head of Jesus during the descent from the cross and the transfer of the body to the tomb. Once in the tomb, the sudarium would have been removed in order to anoint both the cloth and the facial wounds, in accordance with Jewish ritual for victims of violent death. It then would have been placed in a separate place, where it was still quite visible.

CHAPTER FOURTEEN

THE SUDARIUM OF OVIEDO VERSUS THE JOHANNINE SUDARIUM

The Sudarium of Oviedo is a linen whose taffeta weave and dimensions are compatible with what can be understood by sudarium in the context of the New Testament. It measures approximately 34 by 21 inches (526 x 855 mm), almost exactly 1 cubit x 1 cubit + 5/7 of one cubit, and can indeed belong to the time of the Sudarium of Jesus of Nazareth, mentioned by John the Evangelist.

The bloodstains that appear on the Sudarium of Oviedo correspond to what we know about the passion, death and burial of Jesus of Nazareth, according to the studies of EDICES[7].

1. The Sudarium of Oviedo was placed on the body of a crucifixion victim while he was still in a vertical position, approximately one hour after death. The head of this man was bloody, and stains from puncture wounds in the back of the head appear on the cloth. The man's head was completely inclined toward the right, and an obstacle prevented the linen from being wrapped completely around the head. The obstacle was most probably the right arm, which was raised in such a way that it impeded this process. The cloth was, therefore, folded back on the face. The major bloodstains are formed by a mixture of blood and pulmonary edema (in the proportion of 1:6) that began to flow from the nose and mouth after death had already occurred. Pulmonary edema is caused in the case

---

[7] See *El Sudario de Oviedo: Hallazgos recientes* (Valencia, 1998).

of crucifixion by the respiratory difficulty suffered by the victim, and is compatible with the death of Jesus on the cross. One has only to look at a traditional Crucifix of Jesus to understand the position of the head and arms. It is interesting that tradition has always maintained that this was the position in which He died, and this is supported by the studies on the Sudarium of Oviedo.

2.   After being taken down from the cross, the body of the man whose head was wrapped in the Sudarium of Oviedo was placed in a lateral right prone position, or nearly face down, for approximately one hour. According to tradition, the body of Jesus was placed somewhere between the cross where He was crucified and the garden tomb of Joseph of Arimathea. This can correspond to the time when the nails were extracted from the hands in order to separate the body from the horizontal crosspiece, and is supported by the veneration of the Stone of the Anointing in the Basilica of the Holy Sepulcher in Jerusalem. It is also likely that a first anointing of the body was performed at this time.

3.   The body of the man of the Sudarium of Oviedo was then moved to another location, a process that took approximately five to ten minutes. The body of Jesus was also moved to the tomb. The distance between the tomb and Golgotha in the Basilica of the Holy Sepulcher is 40 meters, a distance that would take less than 10 minutes to cover.

4.   While the body was in a horizontal position, the Sudarium of Oviedo was re-wrapped so that it completely encircled the head of the victim. The final position of the cloth is that of a cone-shaped hood or *capucha*, which was perfectly fitted to the head, fastened to the hair with sharply-pointed instruments, perhaps thorns. When the body was brought to its final destination point, the Sudarium of Oviedo was removed and anointed with aloe and myrrh. The majority of translations of John 20 speak of the sudarium encircling the head of Jesus, not only the face. John also says that the sudarium "was/had been on his head." This is supported by the fact that the Sudarium of Oviedo was removed before the body was

shrouded, and that it might also have been the turban that Jesus had been accustomed to wear. The fact that the Oviedo cloth was removed and anointed is substantiated by Jewish burial customs with regard to victims who bled while dying, as well as by the accounts of the synoptic Gospels, which say only that Jesus was wrapped in a linen shroud. It is quite possible, in the case that the Sudarium of Oviedo is the sudarium of Jesus mentioned by John, that the linen was deposited in a nearby place, still knotted in the shape of a hood, which would account for its rolled up appearance. After the Sudarium of Oviedo was anointed with aloe and myrrh, it had to have been left undisturbed for a certain amount of time in order that these substances would still be adhered to the blood until the present day. It is mentioned by the Evangelists that Nicodemus brought aloe and myrrh to the tomb, 100 lbs. according to John (19:39). It is quite likely, according to the Jewish ritual described in the previous chapter, that the sudarium of Jesus was treated in a similar manner. It was imperative to preserve the blood that had been lost, even to the extent of digging up blood-soaked earth.

According to this information, the following can be surmised about the Sudarium of Jesus, according to EDICES. After the body was placed in the tomb, the sudarium was removed from His head, still knotted at the top in the form of a hood, and was placed in a visible place inside the tomb. The body was anointed with aloe, myrrh and spices, wrapped in a linen shroud, and additional spices were placed inside and outside of the linen. The Sudarium, because of the large amount of blood it contained, was similarly anointed, in order to preserve the blood as well as minimize its degree of impurity. It remained in this position for at least thirty-six hours, possessing a certain stiffness due to the spices, until Peter and John arrived at the tomb at dawn of the first day of the week.

It is quite interesting that this is corresponds exactly to the commentary made in *The Navarre Bible: St. John*[8]. In the notes for the

---

[8] *The Navarre Bible: The Gospel of Saint John* in the Revised Standard Version and New Vulgate with a commentary by members of the Faculty of Theology of the University of Navarre. (Dublin: Four Courts Press, 1st edition 1987).

passage of Jn 20:7: *"The napkin, which had been on his head, not lying with the linen cloths but rolled up in a place by itself,"* the authors state that *"...like the clothes, it still had a certain volume, like a container, possibly due to the stiffness given it by the ointments: this is what the Greek participle, here translated as 'rolled,' seems to indicate."*

An analysis of John 20:5-9

John 20:5-9 is possibly one of the most analyzed passages of the New Testament because it is central to the Christian faith in the Resurrection. It is also the only passage that mentions the position of the burial cloths of Jesus, which seem to be of the utmost importance to the writer. Biblical scholars have analyzed each and every one of the original words in Greek, hoping to shed some light on the meaning. Here we will go through the steps of their analyses, in order to arrive at some conclusions. The most important of these is the work of Luis García García, Doctor of Theology in Oviedo, Spain, whose conclusions fully support those presented in the *Catechism of the Catholic Church*, that the linen cloths lying in the tomb *"signify in themselves that by God's power Christ's body had escaped the bonds of death and corruption,"* thus preparing the disciples to encounter the Risen Lord. When John saw the position of the cloths and believed, it was because their position made him realize *"that the absence of Jesus' body could not have been of human doing and that Jesus had not simply returned to earthly life as had been the case with Lazarus.*[9]*"*

First of all, according to Luis García, the three synoptic Gospels mention that the body of Jesus was wrapped in a *sindon* after He was lowered from the cross. As we have already seen, *sindon* is the Greek word for a burial shroud that is large enough to wrap the entire body of the deceased. St. Matthew says that Joseph of Arimathea *"took the body [of Jesus], and wrapped it in a clean linen shroud (sindon), and laid it in his own new tomb, which he had hewn in the rock..."* (27:59-60). According to St. Mark: *"And he bought a linen shroud (sindon), and taking him down, wrapped him in the linen shroud, and laid him in a tomb which had been hewn out of the rock..."* (15:46). St. Luke writes, *"then he took it down and wrapped it in a*

---

[9] *The Catechism of the Catholic Church* (Ligouri, MO: Ligouri Publications, 1994): 167 and 171.

linen shroud (sindon), and laid him in a rock-hewn tomb, where no one had ever yet been laid." (23:53). The Shroud, therefore, was present on Good Friday. It wrapped the body of Jesus when He was laid in the tomb.

We also know that the Sudarium was present on the day that Jesus died. St. John refers to this cloth when he says that on the morning of the first day of the week, after going into the tomb Peter saw *"the cloth that had covered his head"* (20:7). This, of course, indicates that the sudarium was or had been on the head of Jesus at some time on Good Friday. It can well be understood to be from the moment when Jesus was lowered from the Cross until He was finally placed in the tomb. The use of the definite article *the* indicates that John was already familiar with this cloth, and in fact he is the only apostle who was an eyewitness of the events which took place on Good Friday.

García also points out that the translations made from the Greek into other languages do not adequately express its meaning. The reason is that Greek, with its definite articles, with its prefixes and suffixes, and with its many verb tenses, is capable of precisely expressing, with very few words, a multitude of nuances that are almost impossible to translate into other languages. Hence there are so many versions of this passage.

To illustrate this point, I will italicize the points in question in two different English versions. The *New American Bible* translates John 20:3-10 like this: "[John] bent down and *saw the burial cloths there,* but did not go in. When Simon Peter arrived after him, he went into the tomb and saw the burial cloths *there,* and the cloth that *had covered his head,* not with the burial cloths *but rolled up in a separate place.* Then the other disciple also went in, the one who had arrived at the tomb first, and he *saw* and *believed."*

In the *New Jerusalem Bible,* the same verses appear like this: "[John] bent down and *saw the linen cloths lying on the ground,* but did not go in. Simon Peter, following him, also came up, went into the tomb, *saw* the linen cloths *lying on the ground* and also the cloth that *had been over his head;* this was not with the linen cloths *but rolled up in a place by itself.* Then the other disciple who had reached the tomb first also went in; he saw and he believed."

The translation into Spanish used by García communicates something quite different, however. I will present the Spanish version followed by a literal translation. "[Juan] inclinándose ve que yacen puestos los lienzos, pero no entró. Llega también Simón Pedro detrás de él, y entró en el sepulcro; *y contempla los lienzos que yacen puestos*; y [*contempla*] *el sudario, que había estado sobre su cabeza, no puesto con los lienzos, sino separadamente, permaneciendo enrollado en el mismo sitio.* Entonces entró también el otro discípulo, el que había llegado primero al sepulcro; vio y creyó."

According to García, this is the most correct translation possible from the Greek, and in English it is more or less the following: "[John] crouching down, sees that the linens are lying in the same position in which they had been placed, but didn't go in. Simon Peter arrives after him and entered the tomb, he contemplates the linens that are lying in the original position in which they had been placed; and he contemplates the sudarium, that had covered His head, and that had not been placed with the linens, but separately, remaining rolled up in the same place it had been before. Then the other disciple, the one who had been the first to arrive at the tomb, also entered; he saw and believed."

Translated in this manner, the meaning of the Evangelist is clear: the linens had not been disturbed. The only difference in the appearance of the tomb is that the body was no longer there, and therefore Jesus had risen in a miraculous way, unlike Lazarus, who was resuscitated and had to be unbound from the linens.

One of the key phrases here in the Spanish is "yacen puestos," which is not found in the English translations. In Spanish these two words communicate something quite different than the English translation from the Greek of "there," suggesting that the linens are *lying* in the tomb *where they had originally been placed*. When this concept is not expressed, the reader is more or less misled from the meaning of the original text. It is interesting to note that the translation done by St. Jerome in the Vulgate, which remains in the New Vulgate, is that of "linteamina *posita*," which has the same meaning as *puestos*. This idea, however, is lacking in most modern translations.

Raymond E. Brown, in his commentary on the Johannine Gospel, supplies some additional commentaries that can also be helpful. He says that the translation "lying there" is presumably where the body had been, most probably on the shelf of the tomb, and not on the ground as some translations suggest, for example, that of *The New Jerusalem Bible*. Many critics, such as Balagué, believe that the original Greek word, *keisthai,* means that the wrappings were lying flat or smoothed out, because they collapsed once the body was no longer inside. The sudarium, on the other hand, was not flattened out, but rolled up, maintaining a certain stiffness that made it stand out. As *The Navarre Bible* mentions, this could well be due to the stiffness given it by the ointments. The fact that the condition of the two cloths is contrasted highlights the flattened condition of the shroud, which although it is found in exactly the same place, no longer has a body inside. On the other hand, the sudarium is found is exactly the same position and shape that it had been in on Good Friday.

There are three separate moments in the narration. First, John crouches down at the entrance to the tomb and sees that the burial cloths are lying there in the same position in which they had been placed on Good Friday. Second, Peter arrives after John, goes into the tomb, and contemplates the position of these burial cloths, especially that of the sudarium, which had been placed separately from the other linens on Good Friday, and which was in the same position, still rolled up in its own place. Finally, John enters the tomb, and "saw and believed."

For García it is necessary to use both words, "lienzos puestos," in order to be able to express the complete meaning of *keímenon.* He points out that it is interesting that St. Luke (2:12) uses the same word to describe the infant Jesus in the manger. He tells us that the shepherd at Bethlehem saw an infant "*keímenon,*" or in Latin "*positum,*" in the manger, or lying in it face upwards, in a position similar to that he would have 33 years later in the tomb. St. Luke uses the same word when he says that Jesus was placed in a tomb "in which no one had yet been placed" (*keímenos*).

When crouching at the door, John sees with a partial vision the position of the linens in the tomb, but when Peter enters he "contemplates" everything in the tomb, "*theorei*" in Greek. He not only contemplates the mortuary shelf, which John had seen from the entrance, but also the sudarium, which would have been in the area toward the back of the tomb, where the head would have been. Nevertheless, the sudarium was not on top of the shroud, but separate, in its original position.

It is also important, according to García, when translating "rolled up" to capture the nuance of the past perfect, which is the present state derived from a past action. For that reason it is necessary to translate this Greek word as "still rolled up" or "remaining rolled up."

The final Greek phrase "*eis héna tópon*" is difficult to translate, but the most acceptable for García is "in the same place," or in the identical place and position in which it had been on Friday afternoon. An argument to support this is the Latin text "in unum locum" which appears in the New Vulgate. In the Spanish-Latin Dictionary of A. Blánquez Fraile[10], under the entry for "locus" is found this text of Cicero: "in unum locum convenire," which is translated as "reunirse en el mismo sitio," in Spanish, and which means in English "to gather together in the same place." This expression "in unum locum" is identical to that which appears in the New Vulgate. Another acceptable translation might be "in its place." Balagué translates it in a similar fashion: "not flattened like the wrappings, but on the contrary rolled up in the same place."

Another word is also problematic, according to Brown. Many translations say that the sudarium was not *with* the other linens, but *separate*, but the first word might also be translated as *like*, which changes the meaning somewhat. Some also believe that the Greek words *alla chôris*, which mean "but separately," resemble the Hebrew counterpart that means "apart from, besides," and that here they can be translated as "but on the contrary." In this case the comparison of the linens would concern their condition rather than their position. Brown, however, feels that a separate place is meant, and that the sudarium was definitely not bound up in the shroud. García believes that it is quite possible that, while the sudarium was definitely not inside of the shroud, it may have been placed on top of it. In other words, he believes that it was removed from the head of Jesus on Good Friday, and was positioned in a specific place, which according to Jewish custom, may have been on top of the head, facing east. This is certainly not out of the question. In this case, John would be simply be emphasizing the fact that the sudarium had not been placed underneath the shroud, and that it had retained its stiff, rolled-up appearance, clearly visible as a separate cloth, while the other linens appeared flattened or deflated, due to the fact that the body was no longer inside.

---

[10] *Diccionario latino-español*, Ramón Sopena, ed. (Barcelona, 1960): Vol. 2, p 1645.

What is most important is that all of the linens were in the same position in which they had been on Friday afternoon, with the only difference being the flattened condition of the burial cloths. This is what led John to believe in the Resurrection, because the body could not have been stolen without disturbing the shroud and other linens. Unlike Lazarus, who had to be unbound before he could walk, Jesus had transcended the laws of nature. The absence of His body could not have been of human doing, and the Resurrection was more than the simple return to earthly life.

CHAPTER FIFTEEN

THE BURIAL CLOTHS, THE EMPTY TOMB, AND THE RESURRECTION

The final step is to interpret everything that has been said. What does the position of the two cloths – the Shroud and the Sudarium – mean for the apostles and humanity? What causes John to believe in the Resurrection of Jesus? Can we accept the idea that Jesus really rose from the dead in a glorified state? And finally, who would have taken the two cloths, and when?

As we have seen, the Gospel is quite clear when it says that when John entered the tomb, he *saw* and *believed*. The overwhelming majority of interpretations of this passage come to the conclusion that it was the position of the cloths that made the disciple leap to the conclusion that the physical, material body of Jesus had been transformed into a spiritual body, the same body of the glorified Jesus that later enters the room where the disciples were gathered, even though the doors were locked, and who appears different in some way. Indeed, his disciples and friends often fail to recognize him. Paul explains this transformation in 1Cor 15:40: "*There are both heavenly bodies and earthly bodies, but the brightness of the heavenly is one kind and that of the earthly another.*" He continues in 42-44:

So also is the resurrection of the dead. It is sown corruptible; it is raised incorruptible. It is sown dishonorable; it is raised glorious. It is sown weak; it is raised powerful. It is sown a natural body; it is raised a spiritual body. If there is a natural body, there is also a spiritual one.

This glorified state is the same as that described by the synoptic Gospels in the narration of the transfiguration of Jesus, witnessed by the Apostles Peter and John, whose "*face shown like the sun and his cloths became white as light*" (Mt 17:2; Mk 9:3; Lk 9:29).

What is it then about the cloths that made John come to believe in the Resurrection? Certainly if they had been unwrapped, scattered, heaped, or even folded in the tomb, the first conclusion would have been that someone had stolen the body. On the contrary, it is the fact that they were in exactly the same position as they had been in on Good Friday that leads Peter to contemplate the scene and John to declare his faith. The apostles, of course, had not truly understood the reality of the Resurrection prior to this moment, as was to be expected. If the Sudarium had been rolled up at some point after the tomb had been sealed on Good Friday, it would have proved nothing. Indeed, the word "contemplate" is a key, meaning *"to meditate or muse, sometimes in a mystical or religious way,"* according to Webster. Peter, who had not been present at the tomb on Friday afternoon, must contemplate the position of the cloths. John, however, "sees" and "believes." The only logical explanation is that he immediately knows the truth – that the undisturbed position of the cloths can only mean that Jesus had passed through them in a glorified state.

We already know that the synoptic Gospels say that Jesus was wrapped in a clean linen shroud. Why, then, does John use the vague and inclusive word *"othonia"* instead of specifically mentioning the shroud? And why does he mention the sudarium when the other Evangelists had not?

An interesting theory is that of Gilbert R. Lavoie, who in his book *Unlocking the Secrets of the Shroud,* advances the hypothesis that the reason is precisely because the shroud, as evidenced on the Shroud of Turin, contains the image of Jesus. For the Jews, it was forbidden by God to *"make yourself a carved image or any likeness of anything in heaven or on earth beneath or in the waters under the earth"* (Ex 20:4). It was especially forbidden to make an image of God, and the Jews would have preferred to die rather than have an image of God. For John, the image on the shroud was not only proof that Jesus had risen from the dead, but also that He was the Son of God, because only God would have created such an image.

The image of Jesus on the shroud also presented John with a grave dilemma, because if the Jews knew of its existence, it would be destroyed[11]. Therefore, John does not proclaim the Resurrection of Jesus directly, nor does he state that a miraculous image had been formed on the burial shroud. What he does instead is quite subtle. By calling attention to the position of the cloths, using the general word "*othonia*" instead of the more specific "*sindon*," John lets it be known that the sudarium, that had covered the head of Jesus, was still rolled up in the same place. It still had its original shape and stiffness, due to the spices that had been applied to the cloth. It was not like the linens that had wrapped the body of Jesus, however, because these, although they were in their original position, were deflated and flattened because they no longer contained the physical body of Jesus. He then says that it is this fact – the shape and position of the cloths – that leads him to faith. The reader would know, of course, that the body could not have been stolen if the burial cloths, particularly the shroud, were in their original position. An empty tomb means only that the body is no longer there, but an unwrapped shroud can only signify that something previously unknown to humanity had occurred. Through his skillful manipulation of this scene, John proclaims both the Resurrection of Jesus and the fact that He is the Son of God without mentioning either directly.

The fact that the possession of an image of either God or man was considered to be a horrific crime explains the silence surrounding the Shroud for many hundreds of years, and the fact that a bloody cloth was thought to be the source of defilement accounts for the same in the case of the Sudarium. At the same time, the sacred image of the Shroud and the divine blood on the Sudarium is the reason why these relics would have been preserved at all costs, and why the thought that the disciples might have tried to fabricate these relics is so absurd. The Shroud of Turin not only contains an image that modern science is incapable of reproducing or explaining, but that was also illegal to possess according

---

[11] According to *The Jewish Encyclopedia*, the Jewish fear of idols and images was so great that is was "forbidden to look upon images, and even thinking of idolatrous worship was prohibited; if one saw a place where an idol had once stood, he was commanded to utter a special prayer.... It was even insufficient to reduce an idol to powder and scatter it to the winds, since it would fall to earth and become a fertilizer; but the image must be sunk in the Dead Sea, whence it could never emerge." Idolatry was the first cardinal sin for which the penalty was death. p. 569.

to the Jewish mentality of the time. The Sudarium of Oviedo contains a large amount of blood and that was considered to be impure, illegal to touch. At the same time this blood was considered to be sacred, and because it was that of the Son of God, the disciples would have considered it to be sacrilegious to destroy it. Either cloth would certainly have been confiscated and destroyed if their whereabouts had been known.

It is unthinkable that the Apostles would not have preserved these relics with their lives, but it is also understandable that they were kept hidden for a long time, not mentioned historically for hundreds of years. The fact that there is so little evidence of a shroud or a sudarium during the first centuries of the Christian era, which makes some hesitant to accept their authenticity, should rather be interpreted as a sure sign of the contrary. The silence that surrounded the relics during the first years of Christianity was imperative for their survival.

What does science have to say about the John 20: 5-7 and the Resurrection of Jesus?

It is quite interesting that science is beginning to arrive at the same conclusion, that the Shroud of Turin shows us the Resurrection of Jesus. In his article of 1997, Dr. John Jackson, Director of the Turin Shroud Center of Colorado, shares his thoughts on the image formation problem on the Shroud of Turin and presents the evidence that might answer the question, "Is the image on the Shroud due to a process heretofore unknown to modern science?" What impresses him the most about the Shroud image is its resistance against explanation, because attempts to explain it as an artistic creation or the result of a natural transfer process are unconvincing.

The image on the cloth has many characteristics that must all be explained by any theory of image formation. These include: a) The fine resolution of the body image, b) The fact that the image penetrated into the cloth to a depth of only a few fibrils, c) The intensity of the frontal body image correlates with the distance between a body and the enveloping cloth, d) There are no obvious side images, e) The body image is due chemically to a molecular change of the cellulose of the cloth, f) The red image stains are composed of blood, and g) If the

Shroud is draped naturally over a body shape lying on its back, the frontal body image aligns vertically over the corresponding features on that body. Artist hypotheses do not explain most of these characteristics, nor do the processes of diffusion and radiation.

According to Jackson, all hypotheses posed thus far must be excluded, or at least be considered highly questionable for many reasons. He therefore believes that perhaps scientists should consider hypotheses that are not readily found in conventional modern science because the Shroud may present a type of "new physics" that might require a revision of current concepts.

Jackson has developed a hypothesis that is based on three basic inferences concerning the image formation process, which can be deduced from observation made from the Shroud images. First, that the body and blood images were formed directly from a human body that was enveloped in the Shroud, implied by the fact that the stains are composed of blood, and that the image aligns vertically over the features of a human body in the supine position. Secondly, that gravity was a significant factor in the production of the image, meaning that whatever produced the Shroud image must have been able to transfer body surface information only in the vertical direction. Finally, that the Shroud was in two different draping configurations when the body and blood images were formed, because the body image features and the bloodstains are in significant misregister. Therefore, the bloodstains were transferred in the initial draping configuration, but when the body image was generated, the Shroud apparently flattened, so that the images of the sides of the face are several centimeters inside the bloodstain pattern.

A hypothesis that would unite these three inferences is difficult according to accepted laws of physics, because it requires that the Shroud flattened or straightened after the bloodstains were formed and during the formation of the image. In other words, that the Shroud initially covered a body shape, but that, for some reason, that human body did not prevent the Shroud from flattening during the time when the image was being formed. Jackson believes that this, however, may possibly be exactly what occurred: that the cloth collapsed into and through the underlying body structure. This would require two assumptions: that the body became "transparent" to its physical surroundings and, secondly, that a stimulus was generated that recorded the passage of the cloth through the body onto the cloth as an image. According to Jackson's hypothesis, this stimulus would be radiation, capable of interacting physically with cloth.

According to Jackson, this hypothesis would explain each of the image characteristics of the Shroud. Because radiation effects on the cloth cannot begin until it intersects with the body surface, one-to-one mapping between a given point on the body with a point on the cloth is achieved; in other words, the image is well resolved. As the cloth enters the body region, the fibrils on the surfaces of the cloth receive a greater dose of radiation than those inside, leading to a superficial body image. Also as the cloth collapses, internal stresses cause it to bulge away from the sides of the body and at the top of the head; hence, no image is visible there. The effect of the radiation thus described would explain the chemical nature of the image. The blood, however, would have been transferred naturally to the Shroud by direct contact, during the initial draping of the body covered with blood. Finally, as the Shroud collapses into the body region, each cloth point falls vertically downwards, explaining why the image features tend to align vertically over their corresponding body part.

Another characteristic of the Shroud that would support this theory is the fact that the frontal image of the cloth is "three-dimensional," while the dorsal image seems to be made from "direct contact." The reason for this would be that the top part of the Shroud falls through the body region while the lower part remains in place. Also, in the areas of the cloth which fall vertically downward, body and bloodstains would be in register, but where the cloth is displaced laterally as well as vertically during the collapse, especially near the sides of the body, the body and blood images would be in misregister.

Jackson believes that today, twenty centuries later, we may have in our possession an image analogous to a camera that recorded, in the darkness of the tomb, something that no human eye had ever seen. What John describes in the tomb is that the burial cloths of Jesus were seen lying on the shelf where the body had been placed, but clearly flattened or deflated, without the body that they once contained. For Jackson, this is precisely the end condition of the Shroud after it has fallen through the body it wrapped, according to his hypothesis of image formation. He also states, however, that his collapse theory does not explain exactly what happened to the body enveloped within the Shroud, and that this may be a case where science must look to religion for the answer. The laws of physics are still incapable of completely explaining an event as extraordinary as the Resurrection.

Dr. Gilbert R. Lavoie believes that the image of the Shroud is that of a man who is upright and unsupported, but not standing, as indicated by the soles of the feet. Because the blood marks on the hair and the face are not congruent with the facial image, he asserts that the cause of the blood marks and the cause of the image were two separate events, separate in space and time, a theory similar to that of Dr. Jackson. Another observation he makes is that it is most interesting is that the hair of this man is dark in the negative impression of the Shroud, an indication that the color of the hair in reality was white or light blond. If one keeps in mind the dazzling whiteness spoken of in the Gospels in the narratives about the Transfiguration, could this be the image of the resurrected Jesus, suspended for a moment as He passed through the cloth of the shroud?

For Lavoie this image of a suspended man may be a reflection of the "lifted" Jesus of John 12:32, who says, "And I, when I am lifted up from the earth, will draw all people to myself." The very next verse says, "He said this indicating the kind of death he would die," which implies that Jesus was talking about His death, rather than His resurrection. He points out, however, that Raymond E. Brown, in his commentary on the Gospel of John, argues that Jesus' promise to draw everyone to himself after He is lifted cannot be based only on crucifixion. "Being lifted up" must include the crucifixion, resurrection, and ascension of Jesus, which is predicted in Isaiah: *"Behold my servant shall prosper: he shall be lifted up and glorified exceedingly"* (Isaiah 52:13).

If one reads the next two verses, Isaiah seems to be comparing the glorified state of the resurrected Jesus, as He appears on the Shroud, with the afflicted, sorrowful servant who surrendered himself to death:

Even as many were amazed at him –
So marred was his look beyond that of man,
And his appearance beyond that of mortals –
So shall he startle many nations.

Because of him kings shall stand speechless;
For those who have not been told shall see,
Those who have not heard shall ponder it.

Only in Jesus Christ is this prophecy perfectly fulfilled, and by the way in which Isaiah speaks here, he appears to be referring to an image. If not, how could those who have not heard of Him, "see" and "ponder" His appearance, the same words used in the Gospel of John when talking about the visit of Peter and John at the tomb. Isaiah says quite explicitly that He will "startle many nations," and that "kings shall stand speechless." If we consider the history of the Shroud, the words ring true, and refer to more than faith in a Jesus who cannot be seen. For centuries, the Shroud of Turin has captivated and amazed kings, nations, and Christians as well as non-Christians, who are able to see and ponder the serene image of a man on a piece of cloth, still inexplicable after 2,000 years of scientific progress. As Lavoie points out, John the Evangelist says that the crowd, who had been looking for Jesus, asked Him: "*What sign can you do, that we may see and believe in you?* (Jn 6:30)" This image, then, is the sign of the Messiah, given so that all nations may come to "see and believe" in the resurrected Jesus, just as John did in the empty tomb when he pondered the burial cloths that had been left behind.

It is interesting to note that the image of the Shroud of Turin is today a powerful icon in Russia. The Archbishop Severino Poletto of Turin and a delegation of the Holy Shroud met with his Holiness Alexy II, Patriarch of Russia on May 13 of the year 2000, giving him a life-size photocopy of the famous relic, which will be exhibited in Moscow's Orthodox Cathedral of the Savior. Two life-sized photographs of the Shroud of Turin, one a positive and one a negative image, have been prominently hung in Moscow's Orthodox Monastery of Sretenskij. Gifts of John and Rebecca Jackson of the Turin Shroud Center of Colorado Springs, the icons are the object of constant veneration by the Russians. The overwhelming enthusiasm of the Russians for the Shroud was exhibited at a series of lectures that took place in Moscow and St. Petersburg on January 27 and 28 of the year 2000. Unhampered by frigid temperatures and abundant snow, Catholic and Orthodox Christians were united in prayer before the sacred image of God's love, a symbol of future promise for the faith. These events indeed seem to be the fulfillment of Isaiah's prophecy: "*For those who have not been told shall see, those who have not heard shall ponder it.*"

If the Shroud is the sign of the Messiah, why does John use the general word "othónia" when referring to the burial cloths, rather than the word "sindón"?

While John expressly confirms the presence of the *sudarium* in the tomb on the morning of the Resurrection, the presence of the shroud is not so clear. Rather than mention the shroud specifically, he instead used "*tà othónia*," which has been traditionally translated as "the burial linens." Added to this difficulty is the fact that some versions of the Bible erroneously translate this Greek word as "the linen strips" or "bandages," which would rule out the presence of the shroud altogether. Some seize upon this fact to proclaim that the body of Jesus, still wrapped in the Shroud, must have been stolen by Joseph of Arimathea.

The word, however, is clearly referring to burial cloths in a general way for several reasons, according to Luis García. First, St. Jerome, author of the Latin Vulgate, knew Greek perfectly because he was native of Dalmatia, and also Latin, because he lived for many years in Rome. He translates the Greek "*tà othónia*" as "linteamina," a generic word for "linens." Secondly, the word "linen strips" or "bandages" is in Greek "*keirías*," used in John:11:44 to tell us that Lazarus came out of the sepulcher "tied hand and foot with linen strips." Finally, Luke tells us that the body of Jesus was wrapped with a *shroud* (23:53), but on Sunday, when Peter bends down and looks inside the tomb, he "*saw the burial cloths* (tà othónia) *alone; then he went home amazed at what had happened.*" By using the definite article "the" (*tà*), Luke is, of course, referring to the shroud that he had already mentioned, as well as the sudarium, jaw band, and any other cloths that may have been used during the burial. If this were translated as "linen strips" the passage wouldn't make sense. Luke assumes that the reader already knows that he is talking about the shroud that he had previously mentioned, and that when Peter saw it without the body inside, he went home "amazed." The vast majority of versions use the word "burial cloths" or "linens," the traditional and only translation for almost two thousand years, until "linen strips" first began to be used at the end of the eighteenth century.

The synoptic Gospels all state explicitly that the body of Jesus was wrapped in a "linen shroud," while John once again uses the general word "*othónia*" or burial linens. While Matthew and Mark are silent about the presence of the cloths in the tomb on Sunday, both Luke and John say only that Peter saw the "linen cloths." Luke does not specify the types of cloths, and John specifically mentions the sudarium, but not the shroud. It is, of course, the deflated condition of the shroud that "amazes" Peter in the Gospel of Luke and leads the beloved disciple to faith in the Gospel of John, but this is not directly stated. The Evangelists do not proclaim the Resurrection of Jesus directly, but only hint at it through the reactions of Peter and John. The shroud that wrapped the body of Jesus when He was buried is assumed by the reader to be among the "linen cloths."

If we accept the authenticity of the Shroud of Turin and the Sudarium of Oviedo, they were taken from the tomb at some point, most likely by Peter and John, the first to enter according to the evangelists. After the disciples returned home, John says that Mary stayed outside the tomb weeping. She then bends over into the tomb and sees two angels who ask her why she is weeping. She replies, "*They have taken my Lord, and I don't know where they laid him.*" (Jn 20:11-13). There is no mention at this point of burial cloths, and in fact, Mary is convinced that the body of Jesus has been stolen. If she could see the deflated shroud and the sudarium, still in their original positions, as was the case with Peter and John, why would she make such a statement? The only logical answer would be that they were no longer there, because someone had already removed them. While some may believe that it could have been Mary herself who took the burial cloths, or possibly Nicodemus or Joseph of Arimathea, the Gospel indicates that it would have been Peter and John, who then returned home.

The reason that they would have removed the cloths, as has already been explained, is that the Sudarium was saturated with the sacred blood of Jesus, while the Shroud not only contained His blood, but also a miraculous image, a sign of the divinity and Resurrection of the Savior. Both would have been immediately destroyed if they were found by the Jews, but for Christians they were extremely valuable relics. The Sudarium proclaimed the death of the Lord, while the Shroud proclaimed His Resurrection, two of the most fundamental beliefs of Christianity. It is logical, then, that John and Luke would only casually refer to the "linen cloths" rather than specifically mention the shroud, because if interest in this cloth were awakened in those who would seek its destruction, the relic would be placed in a situation of extreme danger. There is no Biblical mention of the shroud after the Resurrection of Jesus, and this can be taken as a sign of its authenticity. The cloths would have been safeguarded within the new Christian community, but hidden from the rest of the world for many hundreds of years to ensure their safety. In fact, the Sudarium of Oviedo, until recently, has been hidden in Spain, venerated by the faithful who were not permitted to actually see or touch the relic, and unknown to the rest of the world. Its presence there has never been advertised in order to attract tourists. It is only at the dawn of the Millennium, two thousand years after the birth of Christ, that it is beginning to be known.

CHAPTER SIXTEEN

THE SUDARIUM AND THE SHROUD: HOW OTHER WORKS TREAT THE SUBJECT

T*he Poem of the Man-God*, written by María Valtorta, is a five-volume life of Jesus, which extends from the birth and childhood of the Virgin Mary to her assumption into Heaven. According to the introduction, the work is a "gospel" that...

...neither substitutes nor changes the Gospel, but rather narrates it, integrating and illuminating it, with the declared purpose of reviving in men's hearts the love for Christ and His Mother. And it was 'revealed' to Maria Valtorta, called 'Little John,' to place her close to the Evangelist who was the favorite disciple. Little, because of the dependence of her Work although quite extensive, on those of the Evangelists who, in short manuscripts, enclosed what is essential.[12]

Maria was an invalid from Italy, who wrote in bed from 1943 to 1947 without consulting books, except for the Bible and the catechism of Pope Pius X. According to her testimony, she wrote from visions and dictation from Christ, as a "spokesman" and "pen." She died in 1961.

The work is presented by the publishers as having been approved by Pope Pius XII, who said, "*Publish this work as it is (…) Whoever reads it, will understand.*"[13] The work is truly impressive, and I avidly read all five

---

[12] Volume 1, Centro Editoriale Valtortiano srl, Isola del Liri (Fr) Italy, 1986. Distributed by Librairie Editions Paulines, Sherbrooke, Quebec, Canada

[13] Osservatore Romano, Feb. 26, 1948, private audience.

volumes more than twelve years ago. I must admit, however, that a great part of the attraction was the belief that it had been divinely inspired, and that it had been "approved" by the Church. I was surprised when, not long ago, I heard that it had been condemned by the Catholic Church due to errors of dogma and discrepancies with the Gospels, because I personally had not noted any problems. While working on this project, I thought it would be interesting to compare the sections dealing with the Shroud and the Sudarium in the tomb, to see if this work might contribute to the understanding of the importance of the placement of the linens, and how the beloved disciple came to faith in the Resurrection. What I found was surprising, even shocking.

First of all, after Peter and John, followed by the Magdalene, have arrived at the tomb, John kneels down at the open entrance to venerate. He only sees, heaped on the floor, the linen cloths placed on the Shroud. John then tells Peter that there is "really nothing," and invites Peter to enter. Peter has great difficulty seeing in the dark tomb, but touches the table of the anointing, and "feels" that it is empty. Peter announces to John that "He is not here." John then stands up and goes in. As John enters the tomb, Peter discovers the sudarium in a corner, "folded diligently and within it the Shroud rolled up carefully." Peter says to John, "They have really abducted Him," and John answers, "Peter, Peter! This... is really the end!" They then come out of the tomb, looking annihilated. Peter and John slowly go away, but the Magdalene refuses. She stays crouched on the ground, close to the entrance and weeps. She then raises her head, looks inside, and sees the two angels, sitting at the head and at the foot of the anointing stone. She turns around to see who the angels are looking at, and notices a Man, although she does not recognize him at once as the Risen Lord.

After her encounter with Jesus, Mary runs back to the house, and announces to all that Jesus has risen. Peter and John rush there, and Salome and Susanna come in from the Supper room. Mary of Alphaeus, along with Martha and Johanna, come in from the street and say that they have been at the tomb as well, and that they saw two angels, who ordered them to tell the apostles that He had risen from the dead. Peter and John, however, are still "very doubtful," and as they look at each other, Valtorta comments that "their eyes say, 'Women's fancy.'" As some of the other women dare to speak, their doubt grows stronger and stronger. Two elderly women decide to go back to the tomb. The other women remain, and are "quietly derided by the two apostles." When the two women return, Peter tells them that they are "mad." He says, "*I can only believe what I have seen: the open empty Sepulchre, and the guards who have run away with the stolen Corpse.*" Mary, the Mother of Jesus, finally breaks her long silence and announces that she, too, has seen her Son. Peter "dares not deny any longer," and shouts that they must let the others know. Valtorta comments that he does not realize, however, "*that again he confesses that he does not believe blindly in His Resurrection.*"

Needless to say, the Valtortian "gospel" is a contradiction of the Gospel of John. In the first place, the position of the cloths does not coincide. Not only do they not agree, but the gospel of "little" John contains a discrepancy within itself. First, the author says that John sees that the burial cloths, heaped on the floor, are on top of the Shroud. Then Peter "discovers" the Sudarium "folded diligently and within it the Shroud rolled up carefully." John sees the Shroud underneath the burial cloths, which are heaped on top of it, and then Peter find the Sudarium, a relatively small cloth, folded neatly with the Shroud, a large cloth, rolled up inside of it. If the Shroud had been rolled up inside the Sudarium, with the other burial cloths heaped on top of it, how could John know that it was there? The Gospel of John is quite explicit when it says that the Sudarium was not with the other burial cloths, but rolled up separately, and suggests that it had kept its original shape, while the other cloths appeared deflated. At the very least one would also have to accept the translation of "lying there," which means that the burial cloths were neither "rolled up" nor placed in a heap.

John also stands up to enter the tomb, when generally one had to bend down to go through the low, narrow entrance. There is no contemplation of the placement of the cloths, and the two apostles leave believing that Jesus had been stolen, which is the antithesis of the Johannine Gospel account. There is no sign, no arrival at faith, and no reason why this passage would have been included in the Gospel of John if it had happened in this manner. John and Peter not only leave the tomb in a state of disbelief, but also continue to doubt the Resurrection after many others report their encounters with the angels and the Risen Lord. The manner in which the account places the male apostles in conflict with the women is also rather disturbing because it seems to present the women as spiritually superior to the apostles Peter and John, perhaps a reflection of personal circumstances within the author's family.

In the Valtortian account about the two shrouds, Joseph of Arimathea, Nicodemus, and Lazarus arrive at the house of Mary to present her with the Shroud, after the ascension of Jesus into Heaven. She has still not seen it, or the image it contains. She asks them, growing pale, if they have perhaps His garments, the one she made, and begins to weep. Lazarus says that he was not able to find His garments, but that Joseph took both shrouds away from the tomb and brought them to Lazarus at Bethany to avoid any sacrilegious abuse of them. After the first dangerous days, they decided to give the first Shroud [the Sudarium?] to Mary, and that Nicodemus took the other Shroud [the Shroud of Turin] to his country house because it was out of town and safer. Mary only remarks, "Really, Lazarus, they belonged to Joseph."

Nicodemus then announces that, since he is no longer a Hebrew and no longer subject to the prohibition of Deuteronomy[14] concerning carved images and castings, that he was thinking of making a statue of Jesus crucified, using one of his gigantic cedars of Lebanon, and of concealing one of the Shrouds inside it, the first one, if Mary would give it back to him. He says that it would distress her too much to see it because the filthiness is visible on it, and because, due to the...

> ...shocks it received when descending from Golgotha, shocks that continually shifted that tortured Head, the image is so confused that it is difficult to distinguish it. But that cloth, although the image is confused and it is dirty, is always dear and sacred to me, because on it there is always some of His blood and perspiration. Hidden in that sculpture it will always be safe, because no Israelite of the high castes will ever dare to touch a sculpture.

While the reference to the well-known legend about the sculpture made

---

[14] The 2nd commandment of the decalogue (Ex 20:4-6; Dt 5:8-10; cf Lv 26:1; Dt 4:15-23) prohibits the manufacture of images of anything "in the heavens above, or the earth below, or the waters beneath the earth." The enumeration is comprehensive and includes every visible object which can be represented. *Dictionary of the Bible,* John L. McKenzie, S.J.

by Nicodemus of the crucified Christ is without historical substance[15], the indication of the confused image of the cloth is contradictory and misleading. It appears at first that the "other shroud" mentioned by Nicodemus could be the Sudarium of Oviedo. Nevertheless, although the Sudarium of Oviedo clearly contains a great deal of blood, there is no "image" on it of any kind. This passage from Valtorta's book seems to indicate that the "other shroud" had been placed on the head of Jesus during the descent from the cross and the procession to the tomb, but there is no mention of this in her account of these events. On the contrary, upon being unnailed and taken from the cross, Jesus is laid in his Mother's lap, as is portrayed in so many works of art. There is clearly no cloth covering His head, because Mary caresses His face, removes the crown of thorns, and tidies the hair. The body is then enveloped in a sheet and carried to the tomb, where Mary once again attends to His head, which remains uncovered. There is no mention of this bloodstained "shroud" in the burial process; the head is tied with a chin-bandage and the heavily anointed body is then wrapped in a clean shroud. Joseph *"lays another linen sudarium and other cloths of the kind, similar to wide rectangular strips, that pass from right to left, above the Body, making the Shroud adhere to the Body."* This sudarium, however, placed over the Shroud, would not be saturated with blood, and is clearly not the Sudarium of Oviedo.

The sudarium mentioned by Valtorta is a wide rectangular strip that covers the body of Jesus in order to make the shroud adhere to it, and has nothing to do with the head. Jesus' head is exposed during the descent from the cross and is caressed by His Mother at the foot of the cross and in the tomb. The only cloth mentioned at this point is the sheet, which clearly is not a head cloth. It is obvious that, for Valtorta, the "other shroud" is not a sudarium, but rather another body sheet or

---

[15] Images said to have been carved by Nicodemus are abundant. For example, in the Cathedral of Burgos, Spain, there is an image of Christ crucified, said to have been carved by Nicodemus. Tradition says that a pious merchant found it at sea and entrusted it to the Augustinian monks. This is said to be of wood covered with buffalo skin, and has been dated to 14th century Flanders. In the *Cámara Santa* of the Cathedral of Oviedo there is another cross said to have been made by Nicodemus, from the 7th century.

shroud. It is ironic that it almost matches the description of the Sudarium of Oviedo, except for its size and the presence of a "confused image." It is not used in the same manner, however, and there is no mention of any other cloth that had covered the head of Jesus.

With all the comings and goings at the tomb on the morning of the Resurrection, there is no Biblical mention of Joseph and Nicodemus, and one can only imagine at what point Joseph took the cloths[16], according to the narration of Valtorta. It is also not clear why Mary would believe that they "belonged" to Joseph, even though he had provided the Shroud and owned the tomb. The miraculous image of Jesus would belong to the newly born Christianity, and it seems likely that Mary would have been overjoyed to have either cloth in her possession. It is difficult to imagine such a response on her part, that they "really belonged to Joseph." Her Son had already ascended into Heaven, and these relics were among the few material things He had left behind.

As it turns out, the work was indeed placed on the Index of Prohibited Books on December 16, 1959 by the Holy Office[17]. It was called "A Badly Fictionalized Life of Jesus" by the *Osservatore Romano* on January 6, 1960. The decree of condemnation was signed by Pope John XXIII. The book has been the subject of controversy ever since, with its supporters insisting that the decree was unjust because they believe that not even one theological or doctrinal error has been indicated with certainty. Although the opinion of Pope Pius XII was generally favorable toward the book, he did not read the entire work, nor did he approve the

---

[16] In the apocryphal gospel account of Nicodemus, Joseph was imprisoned by the Jews on Friday evening shortly before the Sabbath. When they went to release him, he was gone, although the gate had been sealed and the key was in the possession of Caiaphas. While he was standing at prayer in the middle of the night, the house was surrounded with four angels, and he saw Jesus, who had the appearance of the sun. Jesus led him to the tomb and showed him the linen cloths, and the napkin which he had placed around His head. Then Joseph knew that it was Jesus, and worshipped him. Jesus then took him by the hand, led him to his own house in Arimathea, and told him not to leave his house until the fortieth day. If there is any truth to this narration, Joseph could not have taken the burial cloths.

[17] The Index of Forbidden Books was suppressed in 1966, but still "retains its moral force despite its dissolution," according to Cardinal Ratzinger.

text of the Preface, which spoke of a supernatural phenomenon. He also did not give the book an *imprimatur.*

Why, then, was the book condemned? According to an article by Rev. Mitchell Pacwa, S.J.[18], the four Gospels do not give us a biography of Jesus, but a proclamation of the good news needed for salvation. The attempts to fill in the information missing in the life of Jesus go back to the second century and continue until today, and Valtorta's work is such an endeavor in his opinion. Since 1991 he has received disturbing documents and facts about the book; therefore, he investigated it as much as possible, and felt obligated to make the results public. First of all, according to what he has written, the biographical preface of the work presents Maria Valtorta as a sad, almost pathetic woman. Maria Valtorta led a life filled with pain. Her father was frequently absent from the home, and the mother was a controlling person who abused her emotionally. Added to these problems, Maria suffered a physical attack when she was 23 years old that finally confined her to bed, and she began to offer all her sufferings to Christ. In 1943, during the war, her spiritual director asked her to write her Autobiography, and when she finished it, she began receiving 'dictations.' They were finished in 1947, a total of 10,000 handwritten pages.

The decree for the Sacred Congregation for the Holy Office cites eight reasons for the condemnation of the work: 1) Although they treat exclusively of religious issues, the volumes do not have an *imprimatur*, which is required by Canon Law. 2) The long speeches of Jesus and Mary are in stark contrast to the Evangelists. Both talk abundantly, sharing lessons in theology in the terminology of modern specialists, 3) Some passages are rather risqué, 4) There are many historical, geographical, and other blunders, 5) Theological errors appear in the books, for example, in the things expressed about the sin of Adam and Eve, which describes it as being sexual, a contradiction of Genesis 4:1 which says that Adam 'knew' Eve sexually only after they were expelled from Eden. Another error is the statement made of the Madonna that she is second

---

[18] "Is Maria Valtorta's *Poem of the Man-God* Condemned?" Available at www.ewtn.com in an answer given by Fr. Augustine Mary Hedderman to the question of John P. Van der Zalm on April 23, 1998.

to Peter regarding Church hierarchy. The Blessed Mother is higher than St. Peter in holiness, but is not second to Peter in the hierarchy because that role was given to the Apostles, 6) Reasons of irreverence, and 7) The author did not claim to write a novel but the words of Jesus. Maria Valtorta calls herself a "secretary" of Jesus and Mary, and for this reason the revelations she makes are taken more seriously by the Church, which decided against divine inspiration, 8) Reasons of disobedience, because ten years previously some typewritten volumes were being circulated after competent Church authority had prohibited their printing and had ordered that they be withdrawn from circulation.

In spite of this rather strong condemnation of the work, a second edition was published, without the necessary *imprimatur*, which reproduced the same material that had already been condemned by the Holy Office. Official notice did not stop publication, however, and another article was published in the *Osservatore Romano*. It concludes:

> *"Waiting is vain and useless: the 'phenomenon' has already been studied scientifically and placed in a well-noted category of mental illness. The additions to the second edition do not change the nature of the work, which remains a monument of childishness, fantasy, and false history and exegesis. It is diluted in an atmosphere that is subtly sensual, through the presence of a flock of women following Jesus. In short, this is a monument to pseudo-religiosity. Therefore, the judgment of the Church's condemnation retains its validity also for the second edition of the work."*

Although both the first and second Italian editions were condemned by the Holy Office, publication was continued, and they were then translated into German, French, Spanish, and English.

Theories that Jesus did not die

There are two recent books on the Shroud that, while pretending to be unbiased and well researched, claim that the Shroud of Turin is indeed genuine, but that it is proof that Jesus did not die on the cross. These are *The Turin Shroud is Genuine*, by Rodney Hoare, and *The Jesus Conspiracy*, by Holger Kersten and Elmar R. Gruber. Neither can be taken seriously, and it is interesting to examine a few of their implausible arguments.

The first is written from the standpoint of a person who simply cannot believe in the Resurrection of Jesus because he requires an explanation of *how*, which is impossible according to present-day physics. In order to explain these events in terms of what would be completely natural, rather than supernatural, he develops his "startling new hypothesis" about the last days of Jesus, using arguments that simply do not make sense.

First, Hoare says that the *soudarión* and the *othónia* were "*bundled up*," and that someone must have done this. The Shroud, according to his line of reasoning, would have been left along the shelf if the body had dematerialized. One must question what Bible he is reading. Nowhere in the Gospel of John, not in any version I have ever seen, does it say that the sudarium and the burial cloths were "bundled up" and that the Shroud was missing. As we have seen, the cloths were in their original positions, the sudarium separate from the burial cloths. The sudarium was rolled up, while the burial cloths appeared to be deflated or flattened; the cloths were not "bundled up." According to Hoare, the Gospel of John is the least reliable, and he uses this argument whenever he chooses to contradict the Evangelist.

Because it is impossible for a person who had been so close to death to walk out of a tomb, giving the disciples the impression that he was the conqueror of death, there remains only one alternative, in his opinion: that Joseph of Arimathea stole the body and the Shroud. Joseph and Nicodemus deliberately left the body improperly interred, and because "*it would have been unthinkable to have abandoned it forever in a state of ritual impurity*," it is plain to the author that they planned to come back any time after sunset on Saturday. Nevertheless, when they returned and stripped off the top of the cloth, it would have been obvious that Jesus was still alive, and they would have, therefore, taken the body. Rodney Hoare does not explain, however, how they got past the guards who were watching the tomb, and is completely ignorant about the regulations in regard to victims who had bled while dying. The burial was, as John clearly states, according to Jewish custom.

Nor does Hoare present any convincing evidence why Jesus would have survived the crucifixion. He argues that he must have been offered opium on the sponge, and that He went into a deep coma that convinced everyone He was really dead. According to evidence on the Shroud, he writes, the body must have left the cloth when He was still alive or very soon after death. This, he proclaims, is substantiated by the fact that He *"recovered and his recovery was witnessed by many people, who were able to touch his body and watch him eat and drink."* He doesn't attempt to explain how Jesus entered rooms when the doors were bolted, or how He was able to walk only days after having had nails driven through His feet. This is the essence of his "irrefutable evidence" that Jesus survived the crucifixion.

According to the authors of *The Jesus Conspiracy,* whose arguments and conclusions are similar and equally incredible, the burial cloths provided a soft, comfortable layer to put Jesus on, whose body was wrapped with a length of linen that was a *"towel of a special kind,"* part of a therapeutic packing. This cloth, in their opinion, was the sudarium, and when Jesus was taken from the tomb, still alive, it was folded and laid to one side. The Shroud was taken from the tomb because it was expensive.

According to their reasoning, the therapeutic packing was formed in this manner:

> *A number of othonia made of an undyed* (kathara) *piece of linen* (sindon), *were laid out. Over these cloths another strip of linen* (soudarion) *was spread out. A solution of the healing herbs aloe and myrrh was applied to the naked body of the unconscious Jesus, and the body was placed on the length of linen. The cloth was lifted and folded over to cover the body. In this way the whole body was covered* (entylisso) *and the function of a sudarium achieved. The quantity of the aromatic substances in the cloth (some 33 kg) made the gigantic wound plaster so heavy that it had a real pressure-packing* (eneileo) *effect on the body."*

Joseph, after placing this curative packing on the body, then approached Mary Magdalene, Peter and John, in order to explain that he was saving Jesus from death. He was easily able to enter the tomb to take the body because there was, of course, no guard at the tomb. Matthew introduced this element into his text only to "add dramatic effect" to the angelic apparition, but must be wrong because the authors believe that the Romans would not have complied with such a request. Mary, upon arriving at the tomb and discovering that the body had been taken as promised, gleefully ran back to Peter and John to tell them the good news, that the body had been taken. Peter and John, totally amazed, ran to the tomb. Peter entered, and saw the healing cloth, neatly folded. It is only at this moment that John dared to enter, and he "saw and believed" that Joseph had indeed saved Jesus.

The authors believe that *resuscitation,* rather than *resurrection,* is the only possibility, because they believe that the Greek words "rise" and "coming back to life" are originally derived from an Aramaic verb that means "resuscitate." Their life-saving therapeutic packing material is rather imaginative, like something from a science fiction film. It gives a new meaning to the word *sudarium* as a "sweat cloth," and converts aloe and myrrh into miraculous wonder drugs, capable of curing mortal wounds in only a few days. If so, why aren't we still using them? The book's claim that the authors "*lay out clear evidence as proof of their extraordinary revelations that put into question the most fundamental doctrines of the Christian Church*" is totally unfounded. Their "evidence" is imaginative invention, without a medical, scientific, or Biblical foundation. Needless to say, the authors of both books are unaware of the scientific studies done on the Sudarium of Oviedo.

All of these accounts show how the human imagination can interpret the Bible to fit personal beliefs, whether it be an inability to believe the Resurrection of Jesus, or the pious desire to portray the *Pieta* of artists, the Mother of Jesus caressing her Son at the foot of the cross and in the tomb. The reality of the Sudarium of Oviedo is not so dramatic, however. It proclaims, through its copious bloodstains, that Jesus indeed died a painful death on the cross, and that the descent from the cross and procession to the tomb were as humble as the life of the Savior. His face was covered to contain the flow of blood, and upon being taken from the cross, the body was laid face down on the ground. It is hardly a scene that artists and writers would care to portray.

Theories about DNA Reconstruction

While searching for information on the Sudarium of Oviedo on the Internet, I encountered an article entitled **www.the2nd-coming.com,** "a unique science fiction story about the appearance of the genetic twin of Jesus Christ." It is based on the following premise:

The Shroud of Turin and the Sudarium of Oviedo have been studied extensively. There is intense interest in the Shroud and face cloth of Christ. Because they symbolize a 21st century contact with the physical Jesus, these two items remain the most important relics of the Christian faith. D.N.A. replication and cloning are scientific 'fait accompli.' Blood from the burial shroud of Jesus can be replicated and used to create a parthenogenic pregnancy. A genetic blue print exists at the University of Texas, according to Dr. Victor V. Tryon, Director of the University's Center for Advanced DNA Technologies.

According to this science fiction story, the drama of the identical genetic twin of Jesus Christ, Kriss, begins on the 4th of July, 1997, with cloning. The secret birth occurs on April 10, 1998, Good Friday, at 3:00 p.m., but the birth remains unknown to the public until the year 2018. The authors believe that the physical sciences have made everything in this synopsis a potential reality.

The premise is rather disturbing, and makes one wonder if it indeed might be possible to clone the historical Jesus from the remains of his blood. According to John Iannone[19], however, the answer is no. He reports that DNA scientists dismiss it as impossible with regard to the degenerated blood on the Shroud. Dr. Jennifer Smith, Chief of the DNA Analysis Unit for the Federal Bureau of Investigation in Washington, D.C., has stated that such a possibility exists "only in Fantasyland[19]." Dr. Tryon has isolated three genes from the Shroud blood remnants and noted in a CBS special[21] that the blood was human, male, and contained *degraded DNA*. This does not mean, however, that a genetic blueprint exists, or that it would be possible to replicate it. On the contrary, according to the publications of EDICES, the DNA of both cloths is pending analysis, due to its degraded condition and scarce cellularity. Indeed, such possibilities exist only in the fantasy world of films such as *Jurassic Park*.

---

[19] *The Mystery of the Shroud of Turin* (New York: Alba House, 1998).

[20] Reported in *The Tidings*, Southern California's Catholic Weekly, (March 21, 1997): 14-15, 23.

[21] *The Mysterious Man of the Shroud*, Executive Producer Terry A. Landau, (April, 1997).

SACRED BLOOD, SACRED IMAGE

See, my servant shall prosper, he shall be raised high and greatly exalted. Even as many were amazed at him – so marred was his look beyond that of man, and his appearance beyond that of mortals – So shall he startle many nations, because of him kings shall stand speechless; For those who have not been told shall see, those who have not heard shall ponder it.

ISAIAH 52:13-15

But now in Christ Jesus, you who once were far off have become near by the blood of Christ.

EPHESIANS 2:13

M any years ago I read a book about the Shroud of Turin by Ian Wilson. It was captivating in every aspect, from the pollen studies that clearly show a route that corresponds perfectly to that believed to have been followed by this famous icon of Christianity, to the similarities that can be found in images of Christ found on early icons of the Church. When the announcement was made on October 13, 1988, that science had proved that the Shroud was a fake, fabricated sometime in the fourteenth century, I remember that my first reaction was that the carbon dating must be wrong. This, however, was not the typical response. Today I have found that most people have dismissed the relic as something inconsequential, that was proven beyond a shadow of a doubt to be a forgery, and the majority will insist that anyone who still believes that it may be authentic is either uneducated or fanatically religious.

It is perhaps for this reason that I was so interested in the Sudarium of Oviedo from the moment that I became aware of its existence in 1993. Here is a cloth that had gone unnoticed for centuries, partly because it has always been treated with the utmost respect by those who have been responsible for its safekeeping, and also due to the fact that there is no visible evidence of a face. Until recently, there was no possible means of determining its authenticity, origin, or use. It arrived in Spain in the seventh century as the *Sudarium Domini*, but absolutely no one had a clue as to exactly what the word *sudarium* meant.

I find it absolutely exciting that so many scientists have chosen to dedicate so much of their time to its study, in order to decipher the origin of the bloodstains, determine its origin, and discover more about the passion and death of the person whose head it covered. While some may not understand the passionate interest in a dirty, bloodstained, and wrinkled piece of cloth, shared by all of those involved with EDICES, what the results of their detailed and painstaking investigation have already revealed is fascinating, and contributes immensely to our knowledge about Jesus and the early Church. For me it has been an incredible voyage into the past, often painful, but always intellectually exciting. I have been present at the foot of the Cross, I have contemplated the empty tomb through the eyes of John, but with the enlightenment of modern science, and I have journeyed with the relic from Jerusalem to Spain, during a span of two thousand years. The Oviedo cloth has become a part of my life.

Most provocative, of course, is the very strong possibility that this cloth not only covered the same person as the Shroud of Turin – which would prove beyond a shadow of a doubt that the carbon dating was erroneous – but also that this person was Jesus of Nazareth. I do not believe that anyone could seriously propose a scenario whereby the Shroud of Turin and the Sudarium of Oviedo, if they indeed covered the same crucifixion victim, could have been fabricated. Their historical circumstances negate that possibility. That the Church would have cherished, hidden, and venerated two cloths that came from someone other than Christ, who happened to have died in exactly the same way and with wounds completely identical to His, is hardly possible either. And if the Sudarium of Oviedo is authentic, if it did cover the head of Christ, then what interest does this relic hold for our modern generation?

I am not able to answer that question for everyone, but from my own perspective and experiences I can offer the following possibilities. First of all, it definitely proves that Jesus of Nazareth suffered and died on the Cross. While this is obvious to Christian believers, it is currently being denied by many, who propose that the Savior survived the crucifixion, married Mary Magdalene, and had children. I recently saw the film *The Last Temptation of Christ,* which investigates that line of thinking in a hypothetical way. Although it had been initially condemned by many, the story ends with the death of Christ on the Cross. I found it thought-provoking, because if Jesus did not die on the Cross, there would be no salvation for this world. Jesus would have been a traitor, as He is called in the film by Judas. Secondly, the investigation of the cloth has given me a much more profound understanding of the importance of the blood of Christ, not only for the first Christians with Jewish roots, but also for the Church today. The blood of the Savior is the tangible sign of God's love, shed in an excruciatingly painful manner for our salvation. As I contemplated the Sudarium in the sacristy of the Cathedral of Oviedo, Dr. Rafael Somoano Berdasco, the Dean-President of the Chapter of the Cathedral, commented, "It is the heart of Jesus." He then added, "the sign of His love for us." Jesus left us with the Eucharist, which contains His soul or presence in a manner that humans cannot fully comprehend, but the physical remains of His blood on the Sudarium today offer us new insights into His passion and death. They reveal the astonishing dimensions of the love of the One who "so loved the world that he gave his only Son" (John 3:16), as the Holy Father remarked when he venerated the Shroud of Turin on May 24, 1988.

There are innumerable other reasons why the Sudarium of Oviedo is significant for the world today. It is historical proof that Jesus indeed lived on this earth, and died. By linking it to the Shroud of Turin, scientists can begin to prove that the image of the Man of the Shroud reflects the moment of the Resurrection. The contemplation of the bloodstains, for people who are predominantly concerned with material comforts, helps us to penetrate the meaning of suffering and death. The thought that the Son of God willingly subjected himself to the total powerlessness of death leads us to discover the mystery of suffering that achieves salvation for all humanity, in the words of Pope John Paul II.

I found it most interesting that St. Peter may have used the cloth for healing purposes during its early history. The blood of Christ is not only a tangible sign of love, suffering, and salvation, it represents physical, emotional, and spiritual healing for a world that is in dire need of faith in something other than its own capabilities and power. Science, medicine, political structures, and human organizations often have severe limitations, but the One who transcended death offers solutions for those who believe. And why is *faith* so critical? The answer is simple. We cannot turn to Jesus for assistance unless we truly believe that He lived, died, and triumphed over death, that, although unseen, He continues to exist with absolute power over life and death, and that He loves us beyond our capacity to understand. I believe that the Sudarium of Oviedo is capable of leading this world to that kind of faith.

John and Rebecca Jackson have given me a picture of the Sudarium that was touched to the blood of the actual relic in 1988. In reality, I have not used this "relic" extensively, but I can say that it has not failed. The first time I used it was after our daughter's surgery for facial paralysis last November. It had been a very stressful week, and for six days I felt pressure in my head, similar to what one might experience in an airplane, but worse. It was continuous, and I didn't know what to do, because it was not a typical sort of complaint, easily cured with a visit to the doctor. In desperation, I decided to touch the picture of the Sudarium to my head, and the pressure immediately left. The second time was when I had just started to write this book the following February. I have had tendonitis in my right wrist, which was also seriously fractured about ten years ago. This wrist began to bother me so much that I was having difficulty lifting things. The pain and weakness worsened over the course of two weeks, and I began to doubt that I would be able to use the computer enough to write. Again I decided to touch the picture of the Sudarium to my wrist, and the pain promptly disappeared. In the subsequent months I have not had a single recurrence of pain or weakness, which I believe is for the first time in twenty years.

Encouraged by these happenings, just before I left for Spain in June I used it once again. I must emphasize that I am not a faith healer, and never have been. Although I believe that Jesus is capable of healing anything and anyone, like many, sometimes I doubt that He will. This, however, was a desperate case. I was about to be inducted as president of the Altar and Rosary Society, and the woman who was to be the vice-president announced to the Board only three days before the ceremony that she had just found out that she had cancer. It had started out as cancer of the ovaries, but had spread to the spleen, intestines, and liver. She was scheduled for surgery the following week, and the outcome didn't look good. I had the opportunity to see her on Sunday at the Spring Luncheon and Induction of Officers. I must admit that I hesitated, because I didn't want to give someone false hope, but the sermon that day, the feast of Pentecost, was about how every Christian has the capability of healing in the name of Christ. Encouraged by these words, I decided to give it a try. As it didn't seem quite right to simply touch a picture to this woman, I decided to write a prayer that we could recite together. She continued to pray until the day of surgery, and I want to emphasize that many others also prayed for her, not only the entire parish, but also many prayer groups. She received the Sacrament of the Sick from the pastor before surgery, and had complete confidence that Jesus would heal her if it were His will to do so. I was in the Cathedral of Oviedo the day before surgery, and prayed for her in the Holy Chamber. I am very happy to report that Barbara is doing fine.

The doctors felt that they were able to remove 95% of the cancer, and that the rest would be easily taken care of with chemotherapy. At the present time, she looks and feels wonderful. The chemotherapy treatments have not caused fatigue, the remaining cancer has nearly disappeared, and she returned to work less than two months after surgery.

I had been told that the Sudarium would be exposed this year for the Millennium, just as the Shroud of Turin. This, however, has not come to pass, and I believe that tradition, a very deep respect for this relic, and concern for its safety have prevailed over the desire to permit the public to see it for an extended period of time, which would have been a unique event in its two-thousand year history. Once again, it underscores the reality of the Sudarium throughout its permanence in Oviedo: it has never been exploited in any way, nor used to attract pilgrims. This relic has been hidden from public view, and venerated as one of the authentic burial cloths of Jesus. Pilgrims suffered many hardships to come to the Cathedral, in spite of the fact that they could not contemplate the cloth directly.

The day my husband and I landed in Madrid, we immediately drove to Benavente, a town about halfway to Oviedo. The following morning we drove to Monsacro, the mountain where it is believed that the relics were hidden for at least fifty years, during the period immediately after the invasion of the Moors in 711 AD. I wanted to take pictures of the hermitages on the summit, and persuaded my husband to undertake the climb, which proved to be much more difficult than either one of us had imagined. We were completely unprepared, were still suffering from jet lag, and did not even have a bottle of water with us. Because we started the climb from the road which was perhaps halfway up the side of the mountain, I imagined that the walk was fairly easy, and that it would take us no more than forty-five minutes each way. I was wrong. It was a four-hour excursion along a path that was quite dangerous due to the loose stones that made it necessary to step very carefully in order to avoid a serious fall. The only reason that we didn't turn back was because we didn't know exactly how far it was, and because I was determined to take some pictures. The day was unusually clear for Oviedo, and I also feared that if we came back to the mountain in a day or two, we would not be so fortunate.

I arrived at the summit before my husband, and was terrified to discover that it was populated by cows and bulls, and some of them did not seem to be pleased that I had invaded their territory. I approached the lower hermitage with great trepidation, and to my dismay discovered that the upper hermitage was much farther, at least another half hour's walk. Since at that point I did not know the whereabouts of my husband, I decided to turn back. The only images of bulls I have are those at Pamplona; in fact, when I visited this famous city several years ago for the Running of the Bulls, I witnessed a particularly tragic accident in which an American was killed.

My husband, however, was almost at the top, so together we returned to the summit. He wasn't about to be intimidated by the animals, so with sticks in hand for protection, we approached the lower hermitage from the front, in spite of the angry bellowing of the bull that seemed to be protecting it. Just as mentioned in the chapter on Monsacro, the summit is also covered with thistles, which can be quite painful. We then walked the distance to the upper hermitage, where the relics were hidden. This church is nestled in the mountain, nearly invisible to the outside world. I can definitely say that it would have been a perfect place to hide something of great importance. The spot is inaccessible for most of the year, the climb is difficult, and the relics were hidden underground, in the chamber known as the "Well of St. Toribio." The hermitage cannot be seen from anywhere except this part of the summit. It appears that both chapels have been recently restored, and they are kept locked.

We also visited the Monastery of St. Toribio in Liébana, for the third time. This is the Jubilee year for the Monastery, which is in a beautiful location in Picos de Europa, the mountains that lie to the east of Oviedo, now a national park. Once again I was able to see and kiss the relic of the True Cross. While the legend of St. Toribio bringing back the fragment of the Cross in the fifth century appears to be rather dubious, I do not doubt the authenticity of this relic. Its history, cult, and tradition in Liébana are truly impressive, as are the studies that have been carried out. Like the Sudarium, it has been hidden in a remote location, surrounded by a tradition of indulgences, constant veneration, and profound respect. A pilgrimage to the Monastery is well worth the effort, and it is easily accessible by car.

As stated at the beginning, this book has been a quest for information about a cloth of great significance for the world. The results have certainly exceeded my expectations, and it is my desire that the reader will find something of interest and value in these pages. I am deeply grateful to EDICES for having undertaken the study of the cloth, and to the Spanish Center of Sindonology for being so willing to share their investigation with the world.

CHRONOLOGY

33   Most likely year of the crucifixion of Jesus, during the governorship of Pontius Pilate (27-36 AD). Friday, April 3rd, the 14th of Nisan, is the most probable date, because there was a partial eclipse of the Passover moon which would have been considered one of the "dreadful signs" of the heavens, mentioned in the *Acts of the Apostles*, 2:16-20. The burial cloths of Jesus are thought to have been preserved by the Apostles. Ian Wilson believes that it is possible that the Shroud was immediately taken from Jerusalem to Edessa (today Urfa, in eastern Turkey) at the invitation of the city's ruler Abgar V. The disciple of Jesus, called Thaddaeus or Addai, brought with him a cloth miraculously imprinted with Jesus's likeness, according to some versions, and not only healed Abgar of a disease, but also converted many of the citizens of Edessa to Christianity. The Sudarium, however, is shrouded in secrecy during this period, a fact that is supported by Jewish customs and attitudes concerning blood. It is believed that it was first in the possession of St. Peter, and Isodad of Merv mentions that this Apostle used it as a healing cloth. It is not mentioned by the pilgrim Egeria in the fourth century as being venerated by pilgrims, but another source indicates that it was kept in a cave near the River Jordan, safeguarded by seven nuns. Tradition and historical documents strongly maintain that the cloth left Jerusalem during the Persian invasion of 614.

381   Date of Egeria's travels in the Holy Land. She reports seeing the True Cross displayed for veneration by the faithful, but does not mention the burial cloths of Jesus.

447   According to Spanish legend, St. Toribio of Astorga brings back from Jerusalem the largest fragment of the True Cross in the world, along with other relics of the Passion. These relics are not inventoried in the Monastery of Liébana, however, until the year 1316. The only historical evidence of the Cross in Spain prior to that date is the mention of a fragment of the Cross in the inventory carried out by Alfonso VI in Oviedo in 1075. This fragment is no longer venerated in Oviedo, and it appears likely that it arrived in Spain at a much later date, was venerated in Oviedo for some time, and was subsequently taken to Liébana. Arculf reports seeing the three major pieces of the True Cross in Constantinople in the second half of the seventh century.

614   The Persians invade Jerusalem and raze the Church of the Holy Sepulcher to the ground. The Sudarium left the city for Alexandria in Egypt shortly before the invasion, but the True Cross was seized by the Persians and taken to their capital of Ctesiphon.

615   The Sudarium leaves Alexandria for Spain in a chest filled with of relics, most likely traveling by sea.

616   The Sudarium enters Spain at Cartagena and is taken to Seville and placed in the custody of St. Isidore, Doctor of the Church.

627   The True Cross is returned by the Persians, bringing about the institution of the Feast of the Holy Cross on September 14th.

657   The Sudarium is taken to Toledo at some point after the death of St. Isidore in 636. When St. Ildephonsus assumes his duties as bishop of the new center of Christianity in Spain, the chest of relics has already arrived.

670   Possible date of the pilgrimage to Jerusalem by the bishop Arculf, who describes seeing a "sudarium" displayed in Jerusalem. He also reports seeing the three pieces of the True Cross in Constantinople, the crossbeam and the vertical bar in two pieces. This "sudarium" is possibly a second shroud covered with bloodstains, approximately eight feet long, that may have gone to France and was later destroyed during the French Revolution.

Its description does not match that of either the Shroud of Turin or the Sudarium of Oviedo.

711   The Arab invasion of Spain. The Sudarium leaves Toledo and is hidden in the mountains near Oviedo in the extreme north of Spain, close to the site of the beginning of the Reconquest, on a sacred mountain called Monsacro.

722   Battle of Covadonga and the establishment of an independent Christian realm in Asturias.

761   The *Arca Santa* is placed in the primitive Monastery of San Vicente on the hill of Oviedo, without anyone knowing the contents of the chest.

791   King Alfonso II, the Chaste, begins his reign in Asturias.

808   The Cross of Angels is said to have been made by angels for the chaste king Alfonso. Now part of Oviedo's coat of arms and the flag of the Principality of Asturias, the Cross of Angels, along with the Cross of Victory, quickly became an integral part of the region's identity.

812   The Holy Chamber of the Basilica of San Salvador in Oviedo is built by Alfonso II to house the chest of relics.

813   A bishop claims to have discovered the remains of St. James, the brother of St. John, buried in a rural site. The primitive Church of Santiago de Compostela is constructed.

908   The Cross of Victory is donated to the Holy Chamber by Alfonso II the Great in 908.

909   The Agate Box is given to the Holy Chamber by Fruela II and his wife Nunilo.

1030   Bishop Ponce of Oviedo opens the chest for the first time. It is reported that a bright light was emitted from the interior, blinding several of those present.

1075 Alfonso VI undertakes a trip from Toledo to Oviedo, accompanied by *El Cid Campeador*. The coffer is opened for the second time on March 13, after much spiritual preparation, and an inventory is carried out. The chest is covered with silver, and the plating clearly states in Latin "*Of the Sepulcher of the Lord and of His Sudarium and of His Most Holy Blood*. As a result of the growing fame of the relics, enumerated for the first time, Oviedo is converted into a major pilgrimage destination, after Santiago de Compostela.

1345 Alfonso XI is denied permission to see the relics, in spite of the fact that he donated expensive gifts to the Cathedral.

1547 Bishop Don Cristóbal de Rojas y Sandoval, after three days of fasting and prayer, attempts to open the chest. He is overcome with fear, and the coffer remains closed for at least two more centuries.

1715 The Bishop of Oviedo, Juan F. de Torres, is denied permission to open the chest of relics and carry out a new inventory.

1765 Ambrosio de Morales is sent by the king Philip II to inventory the relics of the Cathedral of Oviedo. He describes the Sudarium for the first time.

1845 The Englishman Robert Ford describes the blessing with the Sudarium of Oviedo in his *Hand-book for Spain*.

1934 On October 11 and 12, the Holy Chamber is almost completely destroyed in an explosion of dynamite placed in the crypt of St. Leocadia. The Cross of the Angels and the cover of the Holy Chest are discovered near the altar in this same chapel. The treasures of gold and silver are saved and restored: the Cross of Nicodemus, the great Moresque box of Alfonso VI, the Cross of the Angels, the Cross of Victory, the Agate Box and the Holy Chest. The Sudarium suffered no damage, although scientists have confirmed the presence of dust from the explosion.

1939   Reconstruction of the Holy Chamber.

1965   Mons. Guilio Ricci, an Italian priest and Shroud scholar, visits Oviedo in search of the "sudarium" mentioned in John 20:6-7. His findings are subsequently published, leading to the formation of the Spanish Center of Sindonology.

1987   The Spanish Center of Sindonology is born.

1988   Scientific studies on the Sudarium of Oviedo begin after obtaining permission from the Chapter of the Cathedral.

1994   The First International Congress on the Sudarium is held in Oviedo in November.

1996   The Acts of the First International Congress on the Sudarium are published for the first time in Spanish.

1997   A summary of the Acts of the First International Congress on the Sudarium are published in Spanish by CES in the form of a book, *Hallazgos recientes.*

1998   *The Oviedo Cloth* is published, written by Mark Guscin.

GLOSSARY

Alexandria.

The Mediterranean city in northern Egypt that was its capital from the time it was founded by Alexander the Great in 332 BC until it was taken by the Arabs in 642 AD. It was one of the four Christian sees of the Byzantine Empire, but represented an alien culture in a country that was predominantly Islamic. Before the Arabs gained control, it was taken from the Byzantines by the Persians in 616 AD. It appears that the Sudarium passed through Alexandria en route to Spain, but could not remain due to the conflicts of the time.

Alfonso II.

King of Asturias from 791 to 842, generally credited with saving Asturias from the Moors. During his reign the tomb of St. James the Apostle was believed to have been discovered in Galicia and the shrine of Santiago de Compostela began to attract medieval pilgrims. Alfonso II built the Cámara Santa, or Holy Chamber, to house the chest of relics that had been hidden in Asturias after it left Toledo during the Moorish invasion of Spain. Oviedo quickly began to acquire fame for its precious inventory of relics, among them the Sudarium of the Lord.

Astorga.

City in León province in northwestern Spain. Originally the Roman Asturica Augusta, Astorga was called the "magnificent city" and was an important administrative and military center until its decline during the Muslim period (750-860). Legend maintains that St. Toribio, bishop of Astorga, brought the True Cross to Spain from Jerusalem during the fifth century.

Asturias.

A region in the northern part of Spain that includes the city of

Oviedo, where the Sudarium has been kept for more than a century. The medieval kingdom was established by Visigothic nobles after the Muslim invasion of Spain, chiefly because the area was easy to defend due to the high mountain ranges that surround it. The kingdom not only survived the frequent attacks of the Moors, but also extended its borders to include Galicia and Cantabria, to the southwest and east respectively, before the end of the eighth century. Asturias was the safest region in Spain during the Muslim occupation, and was the birthplace of the reconquest of the Iberian Peninsula under King Pelayo, its first Christian king. He defeated the Moors in the Battle of Covadonga (718-725 AD). Covadonga, originally the site of a cave near the medieval capital of Cangas de Onis, is now a tiny village famous for its nineteenth-century basilica of Nuestra Señora de las Batallas. The tombs of the king and his wife and sister are contained in the grotto, which is a national shrine and place of pilgrimage.

Byzantine Empire.

Originated in 330 AD when Constantine I, the first Christian emperor, moved the Roman capital to Byzantium, or Constantinople (today Istanbul). It was the center of Orthodox Christianity until its final destruction by the Ottoman Turks in 1453. The Muslims took over the territory of the Byzantine Empire in Egypt and North Africa in the seventh century, the period when the Sudarium was taken to Spain in order to avoid being destroyed in the Persian invasions of Jerusalem and Alexandria at the beginning of the century.

Cámara Santa.

A small chapel in the Cathedral of Oviedo in Spain, built by Alfonso II in the ninth century, when it was still part of his palace, in order to provide a place for a chest of relics that was believed to have come to Spain from Jerusalem after the Persian invasion of 614 AD. The chapel suffered severe damage from an explosion in 1934, shortly before the onset of the Spanish Civil War (1936-1939).

Carbon 14 or Radiocarbon Dating.

An accelerator mass spectrometry method used since the late 1940s, especially in archaeology, to date objects. It works by measuring the proportion of carbon 14 to carbon 12 in a small sample of matter, such as bone, wool, leather, wood, linen, grain, etc. This is based on the principle that all living things, as they take in carbon dioxide, also take in a tiny amount of the radioactive isotope carbon 14, which is formed in the upper atmosphere. While still alive, the proportion of carbon 14 to non-radioactive carbon in any organism is about one part in a trillion. After death, the carbon 14 begins to decay, reducing its proportion to carbon 12. The time for one-half of the radioactive material to decay, known as the half-life, is believed to be about 5,730 years, so it is theoretically possible to calculate the year of death, or age of the organism. The method is based on several assumptions: 1) that the ratio of carbon 14 to carbon 12 remains constant with time, 2) that, following death, the carbon 14 isotope changes by radioactive decay alone, 3) that it decays at a known and constant rate, and 4) that the activity of the sample being tested can be measured precisely and accurately. In practice, the method has frequently been proven to be inaccurate, and is normally evaluated only in comparison with other scientific data.

Covadonga.

The site of the defeat of the Moors in the Battle of Covadonga (c. 718-725) by Pelayo, first Christian king of Asturias. This battle traditionally marks the beginning of the Christian reconquest of Spain.

EDICES.

Abbreviation for the Equipo de Investigación del Centro Español de Sindonología, or the Investigation Team of the Spanish Center of Sindonology, an organization of approximately forty scientists who are involved in the study of the Shroud of Turin and the Sudarium of Oviedo.

Ildephonsus, Archbishop of Toledo, and Isidore of Seville.

Honored as a doctor of the Church in Spain, St. Ildephonsus is second in importance there only to St. Isidore of Seville. Although the tradition that he was the pupil of St. Isidore is somewhat unreliable, Ildephonsus was elevated to archiepiscopal dignity in 657, at the time that Toledo was replacing Seville as the most important Christian center in Spain. While scholars are not certain that Ildephonsus was ever in Seville, St. Isidore was indeed in Toledo as head of the Fourth Council of 633, when Ildephonsus was already ordained a deacon. St. Isidore died only three years later, in the year 636. The actual transfer of the chest of relics, therefore, most likely would have taken place after the death of Isidore and under the direction of St. Braulio, the disciple and friend of St. Isidore, who took part in the fifth and sixth Councils of Toledo. Toledo was the site of a total of 18 councils held from 400 to 702, and the great majority took place in the seventh century. It is logical that the Arca Santa would have been brought to Toledo at some point during these years when the city was rapidly growing in importance in the Christian world.

John, Gospel of.

The Fourth Gospel of the New Testament of the Bible, believed to have been written by the Apostle St. John towards the end of the first century. St. Irenaeus, bishop of Lyons, who was born around 130 AD in Smyrna (Asia Minor), said, "John, the disciple of the Lord, who had even rested on his breast, himself published the Gospel, while he was living in Ephesus."[1] The text confirms this tradition, because there are many points that can be explained only if John is the author. The writer is Jewish, appears to be very familiar with Jewish customs and feasts, has an intimate knowledge of the geography of Palestine, and writes in a Semitic style as an eyewitness of the events. The Gospel of John is the only Gospel to mention the presence of the Sudarium of

---

[1] *Against Heresies*, III, 1, 1.

Jesus in the tomb on the Sunday after the crucifixion, leading scholars to analyze this passage in order to determine the reason, which is discussed in the fourth part of this book.

Joseph of Arimathea.

A wealthy Jew, probably a member of the Essene community, who buried Jesus in a new, rock-hewn tomb near Jerusalem. According to the Gospel of Luke, he was a member of the Sanhedrin, the council that condemned Jesus to death under the presidency of Caiaphas, but he had not given his consent. Matthew affirms that the tomb was his own, and John represents him as acting in conjunction with Nicodemus, another prominent Jew. According to the apocryphal Gospel of Nicodemus, Joseph was imprisoned by the Jews on Friday evening, but escaped, even though the gate was locked and the key was in the possession of Caiaphas, released by the Risen Lord, an event that would have made him the first witness of the Resurrection. According to another legend, he went to Great Britain, and as he stopped to rest on a hilltop, a miraculous thorn grew out of the staff that he stuck in the ground. It is said that it still grows and buds every Christmas. From this legend grew another, which connects Joseph of Arimathea with the Holy Grail, which some believe accompanied him to Great Britain. The authentic Grail, or the Cup used by Jesus at the Last Supper, is thought by many to be that kept in a chapel of the Cathedral of Valencia, used by the first Popes of the Church until Sixtus II, who placed it in the care of St. Laurence before his martyrdom. Laurence then entrusted it to a fellow Spaniard, who immediately sent it to Huesca, and was roasted by the Romans on a gridiron shortly afterwards. In fact, the Holy Cup of Valencia is the only Grail in the world whose authenticity has not been proven to be false.

Knights Templar.

A religious military order of knighthood established by a group of eight or nine French knights who vowed in the twelfth century to devote themselves to the protection of pilgrims to the holy places, who were often endangered by the Muslims. St. Bernard of Clairvaux wrote the rules for the order, and numbers increased rapidly, until the Templars became a powerful army of considerable wealth and property. The French King, Philip IV, accused them of heresy and immorality in the early 1300s, out of fear of their power and a desire for their wealth. The order was suppressed in 1312, and two years later the grand master, Jacques de Molay, was burned at the stake. The Templars have become the subject of innumerable books in recent years, written by authors who have chosen to capitalize on the secrecy of the organization, as well as its scandalous demise, by offering hypotheses that are startling, contradictory, and often bizarre.

Liébana.

The Monastery of St. Toribio is nestled in the heart of Liébana, two kilometers from the town of Potes in the mountains of Picos de Europa. The spot was originally chosen by the monk Toribio, Bishop of Palencia (530-540), and his companions, as a place suitable for their Benedictine life of seclusion and prayer. After the Muslim invasion of 711 AD, Alfonso I organized the territory of Liébana in order to create a strategic frontier area in the valley of the River Duero. Monks came to the region, founding monasteries, among them St. Martin of Turieno, which later became that of St. Toribio of Liébana. It is thought that in the middle of the eighth century, after the Muslims had been driven from this area, the remains of St. Toribio of Astorga (448-453) were brought to this monastery, along with the relic of the True Cross, which he had brought from Jerusalem according to popular legend. The monastery was extremely safe from danger and had already acquired a certain prestige in Christian territory.

Monsacro.

A mountain (1.057 meters high) located a short distance to the south of the city of Oviedo between two rivers, the Nalón and the Riosa. It is believed that the chest of relics containing the Sudarium of Oviedo was hidden in a well in the interior of a hermitage on the summit, called the Church of Our Lady of

Monsagro, for approximately fifty years, from 711-761 AD, during the time of the Arab invasion of Spain. Medieval pilgrims on their way to Santiago de Compostela often attempted the difficult climb to the summit in order to visit the well of St. Toribio.

Nicodemus.

A wealthy and prominent member of the Sanhedrín who is believed to have assisted Joseph of Arimathea in burying the body of Jesus. According to the Gospel of John, Nicodemus spoke in the council on behalf of Jesus, arguing that the law demanded that the accused be given a hearing. The apocryphal Gospel of Nicodemus, which gives an account of Jesus before Pilate and the Sanhedrin, as well as of his death and resurrection, dates from the third century.

Oviedo.

The capital of the Province of Oviedo was founded as a monastery by Fruela I in 757, and is situated in the north of Spain, on a hill surrounded by mountains. One of very few Spanish towns that was never conquered by the Moors, Oviedo became famous in the Middle Ages for its impressive collection of relics, among them the Sudarium Domini, the face cloth that is believed to have covered the head of Jesus after His death on the cross until His final entombment.

Passover.

An Israelite ritual described in Exodus 12:1-28 that is a reliving of the exodus of the people of Yahweh from Egypt. It commemorates the "passing over" of the firstborn of the Israelites when the Lord punished the Egyptians on the eve of the Exodus. A yearling lamb is roasted whole, and is eaten at a banquet in which the diners remain standing and dressed for a journey. Blood is smeared on the doorpost to ward off the destroying angel, who killed the firstborn of the Egyptians. It was celebrated in the spring during the full moon. Because the Gospel of John says that the day after the crucifixion of Jesus was both the Sabbath and Passover, many of its themes have been introduced into the liturgy of Holy Week and Easter, and have also been incorporated into the Mass of the Catholic Church, such as the identification of Christ as the Paschal Lamb that was sacrificed for the expiation of the sins of mankind.

Santiago de Compostela.

A town in Galicia, in the northwestern part of Spain. Santiago is the Spanish word for St. James, whose tomb was believed to have been discovered at nearby Padrón in 813 AD. St. James the Great was martyred at Jerusalem in 44 AD, and according to legend his bones had been taken to Spain, a country that he had previously evangelized. Alfonso II of Asturias, who also built the Cámara Santa in Oviedo for the chest of relics containing the Sudarium of the Lord, built the original earthen church over the tomb. Although the entire town, except the tomb, was destroyed in 997 AD by the Moors, it soon came to be the most important pilgrimage destination for medieval pilgrims after Jerusalem and Rome.

Shroud, sindon, and sudarium.

The words shroud and sindon are synonyms for a large sheet or cloth made of linen or silk, used not only to wrap the body of the deceased for burial, but also for garments and nautical purposes. A sudarium, on the other hand, is a linen cloth of much smaller dimensions, derived from the word for sweat. In ancient times it served to wipe the face, much like a modern-day handkerchief, and it is also believed that it may have had many other common uses, as a towel, scarf, turban, or apron.

Sindonology.

The scientific study of the Shroud of Turin, which has been expanded in the last ten years of the twentieth century to include the study of the Sudarium of Oviedo. The word is derived from the Greek word for shroud, *sindón*.

Spanish Civil War.

According to Fray Justo Pérez de Urbel, the Spanish Civil War of 1936-1939 broke out for many reasons. The king had fled to England five years before when the majority of the elections went against him. The newly established Republican government lacked legitimacy and had become discredited by the near anarchy that had been its only enduring characteristic. In the cities and in the southern half of the country, loyalty to the Catholic Faith and the Church had declined to the lowest point in Spanish history. The government of the vehemently anti-Catholic Prime Minister Manuel Azaña permitted vicious attacks on Catholic churches, monasteries, convents, schools, and libraries all over Spain in May and June of 1931, and the constitution of the republic, adopted in the same year, rejected Catholicism as the official religion of Spain, banned religious orders, and legalized divorce. Angry separatist movements in Catalonia and the Basque provinces in the north threatened to break up the nation. Spain was ripe for revolution, and the chief target of the revolutionaries was the Catholic Church. In all, 6,549 priests, 283 nuns, and thirteen bishops were martyred, and hundreds of churches were burned. In only nine days, from October 5-15, 1934, all of Oviedo was left in tremendous disorder[2]. According to Ramón Cavanilles[3], during the night of October 11-12 the *Cámara Santa* was destroyed. The revolutionaries did not succeed in getting into the Cathedral, but did manage to enter the Holy Chamber by dynamiting one of the lower windows. They burned various objects, but failed to notice the archives of the Cathedral containing the ancient manuscripts discussed in the first part of *Sacred Blood, Sacred Image*. In the Crypt of St. Leocadia they placed so much dynamite that the explosion not only destroyed the ceiling of the crypt, but also that of the Holy Chamber, located directly above it. Luis Menéndez Pidal writes that the revolutionaries had confused the Crypt of St.

---

[2] See *Catholic Martyrs of the Spanish Civil War, 1936-1939* (Kansas City, MO: Angelus Press, 1993).

[3] See *La Catedral de Oviedo* (Salinas, Asturias: Ayalga Ediciones, 1977).

Leocadia with the base of the Gothic Tower that they had really wanted to destroy with the explosion. The Dean Arboleya, in a letter written to a friend on October 30, thus describes the scene [my translation]:

One of the most precious works of art, the Calcedonian Box from the year 1000, remained intact on top of the debris, while yesterday we discovered, with the most intense emotion, the Cross of the Angels, a few centimeters above the floor of the crypt, underneath several meters of extremely heavy rubble. And it is hardly damaged... The Holy Chest is regretfully in pieces; the Cross of Victory still has not appeared. The Holy Sudarium was one of the first relics found and is in good condition. We also have taken out many other relics and works of art, generally with slight damage... I expect to see soon, relatively soon, the Holy Chamber reconstructed, mostly with the same stones piously collected...

BIBLIOGRAPHY

Alarcón Herrera, Rafael. *A la sombra de los Templarios*. Barcelona: Ediciones Martínez Roca, 1986.

Alonso Luengo, Luis. *Santo Toribio, Obispo de Astorga: (un momento de la formación de España)*. Madrid: Biblioteca Nueva, 1939.

Alvarez, Pedro. *El monasterio de Santo Toribio de Liébana y el "Lignum Crucis."* Imprenta Cervantina, 1995.

Ansón, Francisco. *La Sábana Santa: Últimos hallazgos, 1999. El Sudario de Oviedo y la Virgen de Guadalupe*. Madrid: Ediciones Palabra, 1999.

Arias, Páramo. *La Cámara Santa de la Catedral de Oviedo*. Gijón (Asturias): Ediciones Trea, 1998.

Arrieta Gallastegui, Miguel I. *Historias y leyendas de Asturias*. Gijón, Asturias (Spain): Cimadevilla, 1998.

Attwater, Donald with Catherine Rachel John. *The Penguin Dictionary of Saints*. 3rd Ed. London: Penguin Books, 1995.

Bajat, Dan. "Does the Holy Sepulchre Church Mark the Burial of Jesus?" *Biblical Archaeology Review:* May/June, 1986.

Barbet, Pierre. *A doctor at Calvary: the Passion of our Lord Jesus Christ as described by a surgeon*. New York: Image Books, 1963.

Becker, Udo. *Enciclopedia de los símbolos*. Barcelona: Robinbook, 1996.

Bell, Albert A., Jr. *Exploring the New Testament World*. Nashville: Thomas Nelson, 1998.

Biedermann, Hans. *Dictionary of Symbolism*. New York: Meridian, 1994.

Bokenkotter, Thomas. *A Concise History of the Catholic Church*. New York: Doubleday, 1990.

Broshi, Magen. "Evidence of Earliest Christian Pilgrimage to the Holy Land Comes to Light in Holy Sepulchre Church." *Biblical Archaeology Review:* December, 1977.

Brown, Raymond E. Introduction, Translation, and Notes. *The Gospel According to John XIII-XXI.* New York: Doubleday, 1970.

Carreira, Manuel M., S.J. "La fecha de la crucifixión: Consideraciones astronómicas." *LINTEUM* 24-25 (Dicembre 98-Marzo 99): 32-33. La Revista del Centro Español de Sindonolog'a.- Valencia, Diciembre 1998-Marzo 1999.

Castañón, Luciano. *Refranero asturiano.* Oviedo: Instituto de Estudios Asturianos, 1962.

Catechism of the Catholic Church. Ligouri, MO: Ligouri Publications, 1994.

Cavanilles Navia-Osorio, Ramón. *La Catedral de Oviedo.* Salinas: Ayalga Ediciones, 1977.

Centro Español de Sindonología. *Sudario del Señor: Actas del I Congreso Internacional sobre El Sudario de Oviedo.* Oviedo: October, 1994, published 1996.
— *La Síndone de Turín: Estudios y aportaciones.* Valencia, 1998.
— *El Sudario de Oviedo: Hallazgos recientes.* Valencia, 1998.

Cirlot, J. E. *A Dictionary of Symbols.* New York: Barnes & Noble, 1995.

Cohn, Haim Hermann. *The trial and death of Jesus.* New York: Harper & Row, 1971.

Collins, Roger. *Early Medieval Spain: Unity in Diversity, 400-1000.* New York: St. Martin's Press, 1983.

Cruz, Joan Carroll. *Relics.* Huntington, IN: Our Sunday Visitor, 1984.

Culican, William. "Khosrow II of Persia." *Encyclopaedia Britannica.* Fifteenth edition, 1982.

Dictionary of the Bible. James Hastings, ed. New York: Macmillan Publishing Company, 1963.

Díez, Florentino, O.S.A. "Ritos funerarios judíos en la Palestina del Siglo I." *Sudario del Señor: Actas del I Congreso Internacional sobre El Sudario de Oviedo.* Oviedo, October-November, 1994.

Dubnov, Simon. *History of the Jews.* Vol. 2. Trans. from Russian by Moshe Spiegel. New York: A. S. Barnes, 1968.

Encyclopaedia Britannica. Fifteenth edition, 1982.

Encyclopaedia Judaica Jerusalem. 16 vols. Jerusalem, Israel: Keter Publishing House Ltd., 1971.

Eusebius. *The Church History.* Trans. by Paul L. Maier. Grand Rapids, MI: Kregel, 1999.

Fernández-Pajares, José María. *Los misterios y los problemas de la Cámara Santa.* Oviedo: Diputación Provincial de Oviedo, Instituto de Estudios Asturianos del Patronato José Mª Cuadrado, 1979.

Ford, Richard. *Hand-book for Spain (1845).* 3 vols. Carbondale, IL: Southern Ill. UP, 1966.

García, Alfons. "Jesucristo murió asfixiado, en estado febril y padeció calambres y escalofríos." *LINTEUM* 24-25 (Diciembre 98-Marzo 99. La Revista del Centro Español de Sindonolog'a. Valencia, Diciembre 1998-Marzo 1999.

García García, Luis. "Síndone y Sudario, presentes en la sepultura de Jesús." *Sudario del Señor: Actas del I Congreso Internacional sobre El Sudario de Oviedo.* Oviedo, October-November, 1994.

Gómez Ferreras, Carmen. "El Sudario de Oviedo y la palinología." *Sudario del Señor: Actas del I Congreso Internacional sobre El Sudario de Oviedo.* Oviedo, October-November, 1994.

González García, Vicente José. "Las reliquias de la Cámara Santa y el Santo Sudario: Proceso y marco histórico-arqueológico." *Sudario del Señor: Actas del I Congreso Internacional sobre El Sudario de Oviedo.* Oviedo, October-November, 1994.

Guscin, Mark. "El Sudario de Oviedo y el Carbono 14." *LINTEUM* 24-25

Diciembre 98-Marzo 99): 15-18.

— "San Braulio de Zaragoza, la Síndone y el Sudario." *LINTEUM* 24-25 (Diciembre 98-Marzo 99): 29-31. La Revista del Centro Español de Sindonología. Valencia, Diciembre 1998-Marzo 1999.

— *The Oviedo Cloth.* Cambridge: Lutterworth Press, 1998.

— "¿Quién sacó los lienzos del sepulcro?"*Del Gólgota al sepulcro: Posible reconstrucción.* Valencia: Centro Español de Sindonología, 1998.

Heras Moreno, Guillermo. "Descripción general del Sudario de Oviedo." *Sudario del Señor: Actas del I Congreso Internacional sobre El Sudario de Oviedo.* Oviedo, October-November, 1994.

Hoare, Rodney. *The Turin Shroud Is Genuine: The Irrefutable Evidence.* New York: Barnes & Noble, 1995.

Hunter, A. M. *The Gospel According to John.* Cambridge at the University Press, 1965.

Iannone, John C. *The Mystery of the Shroud of Turin.* New York: Alba House, 1998.

Jackson, John P. "Current research on the Shroud of Turin." *Sudario del Señor: Actas del I Congreso Internacional sobre El Sudario de Oviedo.* Oviedo, October-November, 1994.

— "Does the Shroud of Turin Show Us the Resurrection?" *La Síndone de Turín: Estudios y aportaciones. Centro Español de Sindonología, Valencia, 1998.*

Jackson, Rebecca. "Jewish Burial Procedures at the time of Christ." *Sudario del Señor: Actas del I Congreso Internacional sobre El Sudario de Oviedo.* Oviedo, October-November, 1994.

Keller, Werner. *The Bible As History.* New York: William Morrow, 1981.

Kersten, Holger and Elmar R. Gruber. *The Jesus Conspiracy.* New York: Barnes & Noble, 1995

Kollek, Teddy and Moshe Pearlman. *Jerusalem: A History of Forty Centuries.* New York: Random House, 1968.

Lamm, Maurice. *The Jewish Way in Death and Mourning.* New York: Jonathan David, 1969.

Lavoie, Gilbert R. *Unlocking the Secrets of the Shroud*. Allen, Texas: Thomas More, 1998.

Livermore, Harold Victor. *The Origins of Spain and Portugal*. London: George Allen & Unwin Ltd., 1971.

López Fernández, Enrique. "Juan 20, 5-9. Traducciones e interpretación." *Sudario del Señor: Actas del I Congreso Internacional sobre El Sudario de Oviedo*. Oviedo, October-November, 1994.

Mahan, Rev. W. D. and Eld. J. W. Damon, pubs. *Archaeological Writings of the Sanhedrin and Talmuds of the Jews*. Trans. by Drs. McIntosh and Twyman. St. Louis, Missouri, 1887.

Manzano Martín, P. Braulio. "Autenticidad del Santo Sepulcro de Jerusalén." *Sudario del Señor: Actas del I Congreso Internacional sobre El Sudario de Oviedo*. Oviedo, October-November, 1994.
— "Sobre los traslados del arca de las reliquias: Observaciones cronológicas." *LINTEUM* 19 (Diciembre 96): 8-10. Revista del Centro Español de Sindonología, 1996.

McKenzie, John L., S.J. *Dictionary of the Bible*. New York: Macmillan, 1965.

McManners, John. *The Oxford Illustrated History of Christianity*. New York: Oxford University Press, 1990.

Meller, Walter Clifford. *Old Times: Relics, Talismans, Forgotten Customs & Beliefs of the Past*. London: T. Werner Laurie Limited, 1925.

Mercer Dictionary of the Bible. Watson E. Mills, ed. Macon, Georgia: Mercer University Press, 1990.

Moretto, Gino. *The Shroud: A Guide*. New York: Paulist Press, 1998.

New Catholic Encyclopedia. Washington, D.C.: The Catholic University of America, 1967.

Pérez López, Julián. *La Catedral de Burgos*. Burgos, Spain, 1990.

Prawer, Joshua and Haggai Ben-Shammai, eds. *The History of Jerusalem: The Early Muslim Period, 638-1099*. New York: New York University Press, 1996.

Riley, Gregory J. *Resurrection Reconsidered: Thomas and John in Controversy.* Minneapolis: Fortress Press, 1995.

Rodríguez Almenar, Jorge-Manuel. "Otros datos históricos sobre el Sudario: Pasado, presente y futuro del Lienzo de Oviedo." *Sudario del Señor: Actas del I Congreso Internacional sobre El Sudario de Oviedo.* Oviedo, October-November, 1994.

— "El Sudario de Oviedo: Cómo se usó." *LINTEUM* 24-25 (Diciembre 98-Marzo 99): 10-14. Revista del Centro Español de Sindonología. Valencia, Diciembre 1998-Marzo 1999.

Santidrián Alegre, Santiago. "Consideraciones de un fisiólogo que lee la pasión de Jesucristo en el texto de los evangelios." *LINTEUM* 17-18 (Junio 96): 5-9. Revista del Centro Español de Sindonología, junio 1996.

Schlunk, Helmut. *Las cruces de Oviedo: El culto de la Vera Cruz en el Reino asturiano.* Oviedo: Instituto de Estudios Asturianos, 1985.

Sierra, Javier and Jesús Callejo. *La España Extraña: Un viaje por los misterios que permanecen vivos en nuestra geografía.* Madrid: Editorial EDAF, 1997.

Synopsis of the Four Gospels. Kurt Aland, ed. United Bible Societies, 1982.

The Collegeville Bible Commentary. Collegeville, Minnesota: The Order of St. Benedict, Inc., 1989.

The Holy Bible, Douay Rheims version. Revised by Bishop Richard Challoner, 1749-1752. Rockford, Ill.: Tan Books and Publishers, 1989.

The Jewish Encyclopedia. Isidore Singer, ed. 12 vols. New York: KTAV Publishing House.

The Interpreter's Dictionary of the Bible. Nashville: Abingdon Press, 1962.

The Lost Books of the Bible and the Forgotten Books of Eden. Frank Crane, introduction. Newfoundland: Alpha House, Inc., 1927.

The Navarre Bible: St. John. In the Revised Standard Version and New Vulgate with a commentary by members of the Faculty of Theology of the University of Navarre. Dublin: Four Courts Press, First edition 1987.

213

The New American Bible. Wichita, Kansas: Catholic Bible Publishers, 1987-1988 edition.

The New Jerusalem Bible. New York: Doubleday, 1984.

Thurston, Herbert J., S.J. and Donald Attwater. *Butler's Lives of the Saints.* 4 volumes. Allen, Texas: Christian Classics, second edition published 1956.

Valtorta, Maria. *The Poem of the Man-God.* 5 vols. Isola del Liri, Italy: Centro Editoriale Valtortiano srl, 1986.

Villalaín Blanco, José-Delfín. "Estudio hematológico forense sobre el «Santo Sudario» de Oviedo." *LINTEUM* 12-13 (Diciembre 94): 5-11. Revista del Centro Español de Sindonología. Valencia, Diciembre, 1994.

Whanger, Alan D. and Mary W. "A comparison of the stains and markings of the Sudario of Oviedo and the Shroud of Turin using the Polarized Image Overlay Technique." *Sudario del Señor: Actas del I Congreso Internacional sobre El Sudario de Oviedo*. Oviedo, October-November, 1994.

Wilkinson, John. *Egeria's Travels*. Warminster, England: Aris and Phillips Ltd., 1999.

Wilson, Ian. *The Blood and the Shroud*. New York, The Free Press, 1998.
— *The Mysterious Shroud*. New York: Doubleday, 1986.
— *The Shroud of Turin*. New York: Doubleday, 1978.

Wright, Thomas. *Early Travels in Palestine*. London: Henry G. Bohn, 1848. Republished in 1968 Gregg Press Ltd., Hants, England.

INDEX

ACKNOWLEDGEMENTS

This work would not have been possible without the historical, scientific, and scriptural accomplishments of EDICES, the investigative team that has been studying the Sudarium of Oviedo for the past decade. A very special thanks to Jorge-Manuel Rodríguez, vice-coordinator of EDICES, for so generously permitting me to use their photographs, for spending hours explaining their work on the Sudarium, for which I believe we both share a passionate interest, and for his enthusiastic support for this undertaking. I am very grateful to all of the members of this team for their outstanding efforts that have laid an excellent foundation for future studies, which would not have been possible if it were not for their extraordinary ability to work together in a Christian spirit of cooperation. Their expertise has been a gift to the world, endowing us all with knowledge about the last days of Jesus of Nazareth and the foundations of Christianity.

I would like to express my profound respect and heartfelt appreciation to all of those involved with the Cathedral of Oviedo, especially Rafael Somoano Berdasco, Dean of the Chapter, who allowed me to privately view the Sudarium on September 14, 1999. Words cannot express my gratitude for the private showing of the cloth to the group of Dr. John Jackson on October 25, 2000, as well as the jug of Cana, another relic of the *Arca Santa*. I am overwhelmingly thankful to have had the opportunity to explain the Sudarium in the *Cámara Santa*.

My search for information on the Sudarium would not have occurred without my husband, Jim, who accompanied me on our many excursions through Spain, often driving long distances in a limited amount of time, and who climbed Monsacro with me the very next day after we had arrived in Spain from Denver. This book would not have been possible without the support of my family.

I am most appreciative to Ricardo Landeira, Professor at the University of Colorado in Boulder and native of Galicia, Spain, for his prompt and very thorough reading of the original manuscript, and for his many helpful suggestions and encouragement. I would also like to thank John and Rebecca Jackson of the Turin Shroud Center of Colorado, for their friendship and contributions, and to all those whose interest, support, and encouragement were essential to this project.